"Edie Kerouac-Parker's long-delayed posthumous memoir clears up much of the myth-making and 'made-up facts' about this tumultuous, but seminal relationship between herself and ex-husband Jack Kerouac. She was there at the first meeting between the Beats, she knew Jack Kerouac as an ambitious, reckless, driven writer searching to make a name for himself in the big city. Honest, poignant, humorous, this book is a must-read about a much-neglected saga of the legendary iconic Kerouac."

—Paul Maher Jr., author of *Jack Kerouac's American Journey: The Real-Life Odyssey of "On the Road"*

3/08

"A qu   n-
ory' b

"Yo
as n
bool

"Edi
than
way. Awkward and brilliant at once."

—Allen Ginsberg

"This is a wonderful memoir of a girl in love. When she wrote it, Edie Frankie Parker was no longer a girl, and her love, Jack Kerouac, was long gone. But Edie, or Frankie as her intimates called her, remembered everything about her brief marriage to Jack, as if a bubble of resilient sunshine had encapsulated those few years during World War Two, and kept intact every detail. She remembers what they ate, what they wore, what movies they saw. Her Jack Kerouac was young, handsome, a lover of fun, and a would-be writer. He stayed so in her memory and though she alludes occasionally to the alcoholic monster that emerged in later years, that creature doesn't live here. In these pages we meet the young genius of just before *On the Road*, adored by all and loved by her most of all. The flavor of the war years with all their privations and mad hopes wafts from these pages freshly, like an Atlantic breeze, and makes one wonder, finally, what might have happened if Jack had settled down with Frankie, instead of following the turbulent destiny that changed America."

—Andrei Codrescu, author of *Wakefield*, a novel

You'll be Okay

MY LIFE WITH JACK KEROUAC

You'll be Okay

MY LIFE WITH JACK KEROUAC

by Edie Kerouac-Parker

I.C.C. LIBRARY

Edited by Timothy Moran and Bill Morgan

CITY**LIGHTS**
SAN FRANCISCO

© 2007 by Timothy Moran and Bill Morgan

Cover photo of Edie Kerouac-Parker © Timothy Moran. Courtesy of the Beats Collection: Edie Parker and Henri Cru Papers, Rare Book Collection, The Wilson Library, University of North Carolina at Chapel Hill.

Cover photo of Jack Kerouac (1953) © the Allen Ginsberg Trust

Cover design by em dash

Text design by Gambrinus

Library of Congress Cataloging-in-Publication Data
Kerouac, Edie Parker, 1923-1992.
  You'll be okay : the memoirs of Jack Kerouac's first wife / by Frankie Edith Kerouac-Parker ; edited by Timothy Moran and Bill Morgan.
    p. cm.
  Includes bibliographical references (p.) and index.
  ISBN-13: 978-0-87286-464-1 (alk. paper)
  ISBN-10: 0-87286-464-2 (alk. paper)
    1. Kerouac, Jack, 1922-1969--Marriage. 2. Kerouac, Edie Parker, 1923-1992.--Mariage. 3. Authors, American--20th century--Biography. 4. Beat generation--Biography. I. Moran, Timothy. II. Morgan, Bill, 1949- III. Title.

PS3521.E735Z739 2007
813'.54--dc22
[B]
                                                    2007025536

Visit our website: www.citylights.com
City Lights books are published at the City Lights Bookstore,
261 Columbus Avenue, San Francisco, CA 94133.

acknowledgments
. . .

A book is rarely the result of the efforts of one person. There arc many people who, along the way, were great sources of inspiration, advice, support, encouragement and aid. It is with a profound sense of indebtedness and sincere gratitude that I note these people:

Special thanks go to my co-editor and friend, Bill Morgan. This book would not have come to fruition without him. Thanks to my "best pal," Henri Cru who took me into his pad, his life and his trust. My agent, Sterling Lord, along with Lawrence Ferlinghetti, Nancy Peters and Elaine Katzenberger of City Lights recognized the importance of Edie's story and believed it needed to be told. David Amram and his boundless positive energy and encouragement refueled me at times I'd thought my tank empty.

Thanks to Herbert Huncke for his friendship, companionship, insight, and support, Allen Ginsberg for his sage advice, Lucien Carr and William Burroughs for their encouragement, Peter Hale and Bob Rosenthal for generously providing photos from the Ginsberg Trust, John Sampas for permission to include the text of Kerouac's letters to Edie, Stacey Lewis of City Lights, Andrei Codrescu, Judy Matz, Robert Guinsler, Charles McNamara and Sarah Fass of the University of North Carolina, Ray Landsman, Richard Hughes, Jerome Poynton, Sharon Ballard, Stephen "String Beans" Kurman, Sherry Turkeltaub, Bruce Nichols, and Eve Kamhi.

Most importantly, thanks to my son, Justin, and brother, John. Without your love, support and understanding I could not have seen this through.

Thank you, "Big E," for being you to me.

—Timothy Moran

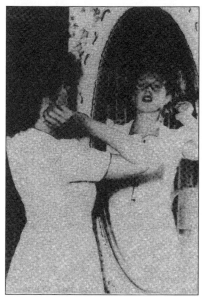

Edie Parker, *ca.* 1942, Asbury Park,
New Jersey

To be eaten alive by time
Is it like a bird that's blind?
To fly straight up into the air
is like life—really getting and going
nowhere
My reason for being
is really the past
but like the future
will it last?

— Edie Kerouac-Parker

introduction

BY TIMOTHY MORAN

. . .

I first met Frankie Edith Kerouac-Parker through a mutual friend, Garron "Muggs" Stephenson. Muggs and I shared a house, but after a year and half, the house was sold and we were told we'd have to move. Muggs found a place to live in a friend's basement, and I took up residence in the back seat of my car. Several weeks later I ran into Muggs on the street and he gave me the name of another friend of his, Frankie, who he thought might let me stay with her for a while. When I called Frankie, she invited me over for lunch that same day.

Frankie was living in a non-descript neighborhood on Detroit's east side at the time. She greeted me at the door in a long flannel nightshirt and blue cardigan sweater with a smile and a small black and white cat perched on her left shoulder. "You must be Mugger's friend, Tim. Come on in," she said. I felt uncomfortable since I was there to ask a favor, but Frankie could not have been more kind to me. She led me back to her kitchen where she served me a salad of mostly sprouts and some "aspraguts" soup, as she called it. I had never met anyone like her; so immediately warm and completely non-judgmental. We sat and ate and spoke for nearly three hours before I told her I should go and apologized for intruding.

Then she asked me if I had anywhere to stay and I pointed to my car parked in her driveway. "How the hell do you fit in that thing?" she asked. I told her it was okay and started for the front door. "You're welcome to stay here if you want," she offered. I told her that she had been more than kind to make me lunch, but she repeated her offer. "Why don't you bring your things in?" she asked. As I brought my bags inside she said, "You can call me, Edie. That's what all my old friends called me." Even in that short time, there was something that clicked between us and I began to feel like everything might be all right. We put my things in her dining room next to an old threadbare fainting couch, and I spent the next two months sleeping on that couch and felt fortunate to be there.

A while after I moved in, Edie came down with pneumonia and was confined to bed. I had the chance to do for her as she had been doing for me. I familiarized myself with the daily chores, did the laundry, cleaned the house, tended to her plants and gardens and prepared the meals for her twenty-eight cats. She showed me where to place the large serving platters of baked chicken, canned mackerel, rice, egg noodles and dry Purina for all her pets. I spent many hours each day talking and laughing at her bedside, and it was during that period that our friendship deepened.

I had no idea who she was, other than Edie. After noticing many books, record albums and photos of Jack Kerouac around the house, I asked her who he was. I had only seen his name once on an old dog-eared copy of *On the Road* that my brother had given me years earlier. I still carried it around in my bag, but had never found the time to read it. Edie told me that he was her husband back in the forties and that he had died in 1969.

As the months passed, Edie told me stories about her life with Jack in New York and the friends who came to be part of that life. I was fascinated by her tales and taken by her kindness, for she had come to think of me as the son she never had. Over time we became constant companions, mutually filling a void in our souls. We did everything together and eventually I began to accompany her to her lectures on Kerouac and the Beats at universities and bookstores around Michigan and Ohio. During those years Edie got up every morning at 5:30 and sat on a small wooden chair writing her memories in pencil on lined notebook paper. Over the years many people attempted to help her assemble these vignettes into a book but they all failed, and the pile of notebook paper continued to grow.

In 1991 Edie learned that she had diabetes, but she stubbornly ignored the doctor's recommendation to change her diet. Within a year, the diabetes began to take its toll and by the end of 1992 she was hospitalized with congestive heart failure. The situation looked bleak, but somehow she managed to rally and was sent home. In spite of the scare, Edie could not alter her diet, and my efforts to make her eat healthy meals failed. While it broke my heart, there was little I could do to save her from herself. At the same time, she was becoming more and more depressed about being dismissed as a minor footnote to Jack Kerouac's life and her inability to find a publisher for her memoir, even though she had been a central figure in the very creation of the Beat Generation.

In the spring of 1993, Edie again suffered heart failure, necessitating four more trips to the hospital. The last time was in early October and it was the beginning of the end for her. I rushed her to Bon Secours Hospital in Grosse Pointe where her heart stopped, but the doctors and nurses managed to revive her in the emergency room. She knew her condition was serious and she was terrified. The doctors said her only hope was to undergo a cardio inversion in which they would attempt to correct her irregular heart beat with an electric shock. I told them to go ahead with the procedure and then went into Edie's room to tell her what they were going to do. I assured her she would be all right.

The doctor gave the operation a fifty-fifty chance of working, and while I paced the waiting room the next morning Muggs arrived to wait with me. Before long the surgeon came in and told me the operation had been successful, her heart beat was normal, and it looked as if she would be okay. Muggs and I hugged the doctor and each other and in another half hour we were in the recovery room telling Edie the good news. We spent the rest of the day with her before going home to get some sleep.

When we returned the next morning to visit, the doctor pulled us aside and said he had bad news. Sometime during the night her irregular heartbeat had returned and there was nothing further he could do. We went in and told Edie, and the joy we'd shared just the day before turned to gloom. Muggs was overcome and left the hospital. He never came back to the hospital or the house. The next day I received a call from the nurse telling me that Edie had gotten worse and had been moved to the cardiac intensive care unit, so I immediately rushed over. I found her hooked up to a myriad of monitors and when she saw me she began to cry and fuss. "What am I going to do, Big T?" she sobbed. "How am I supposed to die? I don't know how." I told her she'd be fine, though I knew I was lying. I pulled a chair alongside her bed and stroked her hand while she tried to come to grips with her own death. I sat for hours watching and listening to the beeping sound of the heart monitor. Edie's eyes were closed and she could not speak; she was bloated and was struggling for breath. The nurse showed me that the blips on the monitor were getting farther apart and it was only a matter of time before she'd be gone.

Fifteen hours passed as I sat clutching her hand and stroking her forehead. I had brought a small cassette player and headphones from home which I placed over her ears so that she could listen to Lester Young, the music from her youth with Jack. Finally, as I stood wiping her brow with a cold cloth the nurse told me that Edie was only a few minutes away from death, so I removed the headphones. I whispered over and over in her ear that it was okay, she could let go, she didn't have to suffer anymore. I thanked her for all she'd done for me and all she meant to me and told her what a truly great woman she was. I promised her I would do my best to see that her story was told. Somehow she managed to whisper back to me, "I know, honey, I know."

My tears dripped onto her gown and with one last breath she squeezed my hand as I bent down to kiss her cheek. The beeps of the monitor stopped and the nurse quietly said, "She's gone."

I continued to clutch Edie's hand, unable to let go. The nurse told me to take as much time as I needed and I remained standing beside her, holding her hand and stroking her hair for nearly twenty minutes. Then the nurse returned and put her arm around my shoulder and said it was okay for me to let go, too.

This book is the culmination of thirteen years of my needing to somehow give back just a bit of all Edie gave to my life. It was a promise that I had to fulfill and yet still I will never stop feeling it can never be enough.

preface

BY BILL MORGAN

. . .

World War II was a line drawn in the sand across the middle of the twentieth century. Just as World War I had completely transformed everything in Europe at the beginning of the century, everything in America was utterly changed following this war. Music, art and literature were profoundly altered, as were political and social structures. Those shifts led to the end of segregation, the sexual revolution and the liberation of women.

The people who came of age during those turbulent times were the people who effected those changes, either consciously or unconsciously. One group in particular, came to represent a whole generation of frustrated, disaffiliated, and discontented young people. Their generation saw the moral bankruptcy behind the use of the atomic bomb and it created an additional dilemma for each of them. They said that they were exhausted and beaten down by the war, beaten down by the conservative morality of the past, and beaten down by the need to conform to the standards of an outdated society. It would be Jack Kerouac who would give a name to his generation and call it a "Beat Generation."

Kerouac and Edie Parker were typical of the people who shared the drama of those global events, while at the same time experiencing much more intimate personal evolutions. Kerouac had the talent to express himself through his novels, but Edie was not an intellectual and she needed to find a much more personal way to voice her own inner thoughts. Her memoirs became her way to convey her perceptions and feelings. While Kerouac searched for a new spiritual value to his life, Parker became more immediate and sensual. She became restless for direct experience and in many ways her choices presaged the social revolutions which would come twenty years later. Edie's rebellion exhibited itself in her freedom to enjoy personal relationships, sex, jazz and excitement. Those things were enough for her, even if they were temporary. At the same time, Jack's search was more philosophical and sparked a new literary movement which honored that search for spiritual values and sacred truth.

Even though the Beat Generation developed primarily into a boy's club, scholars have constantly looked for the woman's point of view. Unfortunately, the women associated with the group were guilty of living their lives without recording them. Most of the women were just as restless as the men. They discovered sexual liberation, free speech, and jazz, too, but at the same time they had to be involved with the traditional roles of providing a home and family. Their male counterparts found it easy to discount the value of having families while they searched for something unconventional, but the women paid the price for their sexual liberation. They were the ones who became pregnant, had abortions or raised children alone and without support, while the men moved on to other experiences unfettered. During the 1940s a woman could not have gone "on the road" in the same way the men did. For the men to enjoy total freedom and search for their own spiritual truths, someone had to take care of their day-to-day needs, be it their mothers, wives or girlfriends.

Edie's memoir provides the only female voice from that nascent period, when the leading members of the Beat Generation were first meeting and becoming friends. A strong case could be made for the argument that if it weren't for Edie Parker and Joan Adams, those male writers might never have met and history would have taken a different course. The women provided the necessary setting, the salon as it were, for the birth of the Beats. It was through Edie Parker and Joan Adams that Jack Kerouac met Lucien Carr, Allen Ginsberg, William Burroughs and other people, like Neal Cassady, who would later populate the pages of Kerouac's books.

It was no mean feat to provide a home for these characters; it took all the patience and resources that Edie and Joan could muster. They were not completely liberated women by today's standards, they lived for their men and their lives revolved around the men's needs more than their own. But they were not merely supportive, they inspired and encouraged their companions, too. They were willing to make sacrifices because they believed in their talents. That duality of nurturing and inspiring was liberating to both of them.

As the war progressed, more and more women moved out of the traditional role of homemaker and into the factories and workplaces previously dominated by men. For a while, Edie worked as a longshoreman and took on most of the responsibilities of providing for her extended family. Becoming the bread-winner was not something she had planned to do, but with the acceptance of that responsibility came a new self-reliance and confidence that later was to become a hallmark of the women's liberation movement.

Edie, Joan, Celine Young, and Gabe Kerouac were all terribly complex and fascinating women whose personalities are revealed in these pages without apology, warts and all. Their talents were used to support the men they loved, but through their labors they grew to expect more from themselves, too. In the end, Edie and Jack went their separate ways. Neither of them ever really left home again, they both stayed with their mothers for the rest of their lives, even though they both remarried twice. As the years went by, they kept in touch only on rare occasions through letters and late-night telephone calls. In his last letter to Edie, written a month before his death, Kerouac ended with the encouraging phrase "You'll be okay." It was from that note that the title of this book was taken.

foreword

BY FRANKIE EDITH KEROUAC-PARKER

. . .

Imagine living under your mother's roof to the age of fifty-seven, a life spent as a captive of both your family and your dreams. Money has always been my center of gravity—a sad, but true fact. My mother held the money, even when Jack Kerouac captured my imagination, and I was unable to reconcile the two. My mother, a tenacious, heroic, indomitable woman outlived Jack by ten years and I lived in her house until the end, just as Jack was to live with his own mother until his death.

If I could restructure the events of my life, I never would have left Jack as I did in 1946. At the time, I felt I had a good reason. The people Jack and I shared our apartment with in New York City were all caught up in the dope scene at a time when I was working full time to support them. They filled their days with drink, music and philosophical conversation, and I barely managed to subsist on mayonnaise sandwiches. In the end, I had to eat or be eaten. Those reasons seem distant now and my memories are only of my love for Jack, a love that predated his legend and fame.

I knew and loved Jack as a sensitive, beautiful man who lived only to express himself and his feelings through his writing. He gave up a scholarship to Columbia University and the certain path to American success afforded him by his considerable athletic talents in favor of that avocation. In my youth I could not understand this, and I was only able to come to terms with it after reading his books following his death. It was shortly after the publication of his final book, *Vanity of Duluoz*, that he called me and told me of his wish that we meet again. In the meantime, we had both remarried twice. Jack had fathered one daughter, Jan, with his second wife, only to reject her. I was unable to have children as a result of the abortion of our son in 1942 and had divorced both my second and third husbands, all the while never leaving my mother's home. After our break-up in 1946 Jack went on to live the balance of his life with his mother, even through his marriages to Joan Haverty and Stella Sampas, the sister of Jack's true best friend, Sebastian Sampas. Through it all Jack persisted in calling me his "life's wife."

During his last years as a terminal alcoholic, Stella took good care of both Jack and his mother, who had been left paralyzed by a stroke. When Stella learned of Jack's plan to have me visit him and his mother at their home in St. Petersburg, Florida, she discouraged it, but after Jack's death she told me how much she regretted that decision.

Jack Kerouac was the fulfillment and nemesis of my youth. He was not a rebel by nature, but was curious and fascinated by those unlike himself, and could not resist the lure of those temptations. My heart was with him always, but my values ultimately led me back home. I was never able to reconcile the dualities within myself. I never will.

Jack Kerouac, Novelist, Dead; Father of the Beat Generation

Author of 'On the Road' Was Hero to Youth—Rejected Middle-Class Values

By JOSEPH LELYVELD

Jack Kerouac, the novelist who named the Beat Generation and exuberantly celebrated its rejection of middle-class American conventions, died early yesterday of massive abdominal hemorrhaging in a St. Petersburg, Fla., hospital. He was 47 years old.

"The only people for me are the mad ones, the ones who are mad to live, mad to talk, desirous of everything at the same time," he wrote in "On the Road," a novel he completed in only three weeks but had to wait seven years to see published.

When it finally appeared in 1957, it immediately became a basic text for youth who found their country claustrophobic and oppressive. At the same time, it was a spontaneous and passionate celebration of the country itself, of "the great raw bulge and bulk of my American continent."

Mr. Kerouac's admirers regarded him as a major literary innovator and something of a religious seer, but this estimate of his achievement never gained wide acceptance among literary tastemakers.

The Beat Generation, originally regarded as a bizarre bohemian phenomenon confined to small coteries in San Francisco and New York, spilled over into the general culture in the nineteen-sixties. But as it became fashionable to be beat, it became less fashionable to read Jack Kerouac.

Subject Was Himself

His subject was himself and his method was to write as spontaneously as possible by threading a hefty roll of teletype paper into his typewriter and setting down his story on one continuous sheet. What resulted he would later transcribe for forwarding to his publisher, but never revise, in principle, for he regarded revision as a form of lying.

Truman Capote called Mr. Kerouac's method of composition typing, not writing. But Allen Ginsberg, who regarded

Jerry Bauer
Jack Kerouac

done in the company of a young drifter from Denver named Neal Cassady, who had a hunger for experience and a taste also for theology and literature. Inevitably, he became a main character of "On the Road," but he became much more — a literary model, supplanting Thomas Wolfe, Ernest Hemingway and William Saroyan.

Cassady had never been published, but he wrote voluminous letters—"fast, mad, confessional, completely serious, all detailed," Mr. Kerouac later recalled — that gave the aspiring novelist his idea of spontaneous style. Specifically the inspiration for "On the Road" was a letter from Cassady that ran to 40,000 words.

The word "beat," Mr. Kerouac once said, was first used by a friend to signify the feelings of despair and nearness to an apocalypse that impelled them to reach out for new experiences. The novelist later coined the phrase "beat generation," sometimes explaining that he took "beat" to mean "beatific."

Earlier, Mr. Kerouac had published a more conventional first novel—"The Town and the City," which was a minor critical success and a complete commercial failure when it was published in 1950 by Harcourt Brace after three years of writ-

chapter 1

. . .

On Oct. 22, 1969, like most of America, I learned of Jack Kerouac's death from Walter Cronkite on the evening news. He said that Jack had died just the day before after suffering a massive abdominal hemorrhage as a result of alcoholism. I was stunned. I couldn't believe it, geez he was only forty-seven. My reaction was strange, I felt that I had to get to him as fast as possible and began to plan and pack my wardrobe. I had a brown plaid wool and suede suit that I knew Jack would like. Shoes, hat, purse—all matching with white gloves and a white cashmere sweater. So off I went to Boston the next morning on the first flight to meet my sister, Charlotte, who lived in Framingham.

"Sister," as we call Charlotte, and her husband, Jim, met me at Logan Airport. I was excited about going to see Jack and I found it hard to think of him not being around—he's still on my mind more than ever as I write this nearly twenty years later. That night I stayed at my sister's, remembering that Jack used to call her "Little Sister." Sister and I planned to drive up to Lowell the next morning for the wake.

We needed a car, and Sister asked her close friend Dee to take us, so there were three of us, dressed to the nines, all headed for Lowell. I drove, since it's the one thing I do well. It was a gorgeous, crisp fall day in October, the season Jack loved most. I was bursting with desire to be with him, but I had to keep my eye on the speedometer or else I would find myself taking off in a daydream.

It was about 10:00 A.M. when we arrived in Lowell the day before Jack's funeral. We drove through the worst part of town—I've often wondered why this always happens to me. We drove through a huge square, almost a piazza, but without a fountain or a green park in the center. Several streets ran into the square like the spokes of a giant wheel. Every house looked as if fishermen lived there—white, two-story wooden homes with small front yards, sparse on flowers, bushes and trees, as if the ocean winds had swept them away. But there was no ocean nearby, no sand or fishing nets drying in the wind. Just a bleak, raw, cold town. However, we soon found the better part of town—the Lowell I remembered from my visits back then and the Lowell Jack spoke of so fondly. For some reason I began to think of how impressed Jack had been with the Chicago "Loop" because of the all-night saloons. He and Neal (Cassady) stopped in Detroit to see me on almost every cross-country trip. They always seemed to be coming from the Loop and were usually still loaded. They invariably had some beat up old car – dirty, dusty, banged up on the outside and full of crumpled newspapers, books and dirty clothes. I would push all of the trash aside and climb into the back seat with their suitcases. Neal used an old hard-sided bag and Jack had his merchant marine duffel bags. The radio was always on full blast. If Jack turned it down to talk, Neal turned it right back up again. Once, I remember, they arrived in a two-toned Hudson—black on the bottom, silver on top—with four doors. The front shocks were broken so it felt like you were in a boat on rough water—it was a kick to ride in it.

Neal was obsessed with sex and would never pass up an opportunity to mention something about it. Jack would scowl at him and the subject then would turn to money, especially, did I have any? Which sometimes I did. Could they borrow some was always the next question. If possible, I was generous, knowing it would keep them coming back to Grosse Pointe to see me. They liked to stay at the Savarine Hotel on Jefferson Avenue downtown, about a mile and a half away. One reason they really loved it was because a lot of the Detroit Tiger baseball players lived there, and Jack loved baseball. Jefferson Avenue was also lined with all-night movie theaters and bars filled with three shifts of autoworkers per day. When he didn't have the money for a room, Jack spent some long nights in those theaters.

This was my fourth visit to Lowell and the only one without Jack by my side. We came upon a cluster of funeral parlors all on the same block, with black and white block-letter signs in front of each. We spotted the Archambault Funeral Home and there, right across the street, was a parking space, as if it had been left for us by some invisible guardian angel. I sat for a few minutes after we parked, letting all of my thoughts fly back into their hive. I did my lips, combed my hair, held my breath, stepped out of the car and walked toward the funeral home.

In the car I had told my sister that I was not going to tell anyone who I was. I knew for sure that Lucien Carr, William Burroughs and Allen Ginsberg would be there, and after all these years I would be with my family again. I proudly held my head up high. Jack had finally become the famous author we had dreamed he would turn into when we walked, holding hands, looking in the bookstore windows along Fifth Avenue twenty-five years earlier. I've never wished for anything for myself, but Jack and I dreamed about his success. All of my wishes had been for him. He was the genius, the writer. That is how I always felt.

Now Jack was waiting for me inside. Even if he couldn't hold me and look at me with love in his eyes, he was there waiting, my "eternal old man," as he called himself. As we both grew older, death weighed more and more on Jack's broad, brooding shoulders. He told me to accept death as if it were a friend who was coming over for a drink. I always ignored the whole subject.

We entered a rather long, wide hall with worn out, color-less carpeting. Sliding doors separated the large rooms and the ones to the left were open. A row of chairs lined the walls on the left and right. They were the ugly gray, metal fold-up kind used in schools when there weren't any real seats left, very depressing. A church podium with a large register book stood at the entrance, but there weren't any people. Nothing but a black sign with white pushpin letters that read "Jack Kerouac" and the time of the funeral. One of the funeral directors came over and told me the plane bringing Jack's body from Florida had been delayed by a hurricane, so we left without seeing anyone and went back to Charlotte's house for the night.

The next day we set out for Lowell again, this time in a pouring rain; the storm that had delayed Jack was now upon us. It made an already sad trip, more so. Dee picked us up for what would be a very tense ride. Leaves on the road made it slippery and the wet road added about an hour to the trip. We finally got there about 11:00 A.M.

This day there were people all over the place. I took a quick look around but recognized no one. We walked into the larger of the parlors, with those gray folding chairs now lining three walls. He was there at the front, lying in a casket placed on a funeral gurney about two feet high, disguised by a velvet skirt. Jack was enveloped in white satin with a white satin pillow beneath his head. A string of rosary beads around his hands seemed inappropriate, since I had never known him to own or say the rosary. It was not my Jack lying there; I mean, it was, but it wasn't. Seeing him in a black and white check sport jacket with a white, button-down oxford dress shirt and bow tie made me think of the time Lucien, Jack and I had gone to Brooks Brothers to buy Jack his first black and white check jacket. I remembered walking through Morningside Park, Jack in that sport coat, on our way to Harlem to listen to the great jazz artists making the scene: Billie Holiday, Dizzy Gillespie, Miles Davis, Thelonius Monk and Charlie Parker.

Where was Lucien, I wondered? He wasn't there. As I regained my composure, I realized that everyone in the room was staring at us. All of the old Greek women sat along the far wall dressed in long black shrouds down to their ankles, with thick textured black stockings and what appeared to be soft, ballet-style shoes. They fingered rosary beads in their strong domestic hands while repeating their grief in whispered Greek moans.

On the other side of the room two young people, shoeless with worn leather vests and leather knapsacks, prayed in silence. There was no one who even resembled anyone from my past. I stood up and decided to go over to the podium by the door and sign my name in the register book—"Frankie Edith Parker, Grosse Pointe, Michigan." Just then, a very tall, handsome man rushed over to me and introduced himself as Tony Sampas, Jack's brother-in-law and friend. Tony welcomed me and said, "Jack spoke of you often. I would like to introduce you to Stella, Jack's widow." He took Sister and me over to Stella, who was also in black but not quite as severely dressed as the other mourners. Stella was wonderful and so was Tony. They were very pleased that we had come and invited us back to their mother's house on Stevens Road. Tony said he would show us the way to the church when the time came.

Before long, Allen Ginsberg came in with Gregory Corso and Peter Orlovsky. Allen was all hair with sandals, no socks, and a lute. He walked over and kissed Sister and me and recited a prayer to us with his hands clasped tight. I was comforted by his presence. At that time I didn't know Gregory or Peter. "Where's Lucien and Willy B.?" I asked Allen. He told me that Lucien was so upset by the news that he had almost bitten his tongue off and could not make the trip. I never did hear where Burroughs was. Of all the people Jack and I knew back at Columbia and his friends I had met in Lowell, no one, with the exception of Allen, showed up. There were only profiteers and media.

As I sat there in my sadness I wrote, "The larks are awake outside your window but you, my darling, are asleep and can't hear. Rest from your all night writing and birdless birdnote madness. Join all of your cats and come back to me when you are in port from your journey. I will be in the apartment of our youth and it will be the same as before." I smiled to myself. I knew Jack was watching me as he always had and I felt proud that he had accomplished what he said he would.

It was time to move on to the church, so I went back to the casket to see Jack one last time. He was so still, yet I was somehow expecting him to say something, as if this wasn't really happening. Lying on top of the closed end of the casket was a large spray of roses in the shape of a heart—white on the outside and red in the middle. Across the center, a white ribbon read, "Guard the Heart" and another ribbon hung to the side, "From Lucien, Bill, John, Allen and Robert." Years later, after reading Jack's books, I recognize their sentiment derived from the last chorus of Jack's *Mexico City Blues*:

"Stop the murder and the suicide!
   All's well
    I am the Guard"

Sister, Dee and I sat in our car waiting for the funeral procession to begin. A small white flag with a magnetized base had been placed on the fender of each car. At the head of the line were three black Cadillacs and a large limo with the Massachusetts state seal emblazoned on the door. Tony got into the driver's seat and pulled our car up behind the others, and off we went. It seemed a short ride to the church. St. Jean Baptiste Cathedral is right in the main part of Lowell with lots of heavy traffic going by. Policemen directed us to a parking area, which was a long way from the church, but fortunately the rain had almost stopped. As we walked I again had a feeling of pride. I held my head up, not seeing anything, only feeling. I wasn't sad, but proud of Jack and relieved to be there with him.

St. Jean Baptiste Cathedral is immense. The inside was cool, bordering on cold—as most large stone structures tend to be. The wooden benches were worn, but welcoming. We sat on the aisle about halfway up the left side. The altar spanned the width of the church, one step above floor level, with pale marble columns and beautiful elongated stained glass windows beyond. It was an impressive sight. They brought Jack in. Allen was a pallbearer; the other five were people I didn't know—New York businessmen probably, merchants, not a playboy among them. Everything was gray, black and bronze. My back was to most of the people there, but I didn't see any of the friends of our youth—only Allen. I looked for G.J., George J. Apostolos, Jack's boyhood friend from Lowell, who we'd stayed with on one of our visits there together. But almost thirty years had passed and he wasn't there. The last time I saw him he was in bell-bottoms and a pea coat. Jack and I had taken him to the train station in Lowell on his way to his navy job in Boston.

The service began and a very young priest gave a eulogy over Jack's casket. It seemed that he and Jack had been friends. He had loaned many books to Jack and they discussed them after Jack read them. I was a good listener and always tried to read whatever Jack recommended. He boasted, "Kerouac educated, you are." The eulogy was very long and I couldn't concentrate on it. I decided that I would read it in the paper the next day. At last the service mercifully came to an end. Allen turned and smiled at me—a very sweet thing to do—he knew what I was feeling. We, all of us, were and always will be very close, and a big part of us was lying in that casket.

We followed the procession out of the church, back into the cold, crisp air, and walked to the car in silence. Tony wasn't with us this time as we followed the hearse to Edson Cemetery. Again we were forced to park quite a distance from the gravesite and walk across grassy fields. As we approached, my heart stopped. There ahead of me a young man walked—the same broad shoulders, same swinging walk, same hands in his pockets and shiny, gorgeous black hair that Jack had twenty years ago. But he never looked at me, and I realized he must have been a cousin of Jack's. The Kerouacs were from nearby Nashua, New Hampshire. That made me wonder. Why wasn't Jack being buried with his family, in Nashua? His father, Leo, and brother, Gerard, are buried there. And his mother, Gabe, would be also.

A small tan and green tent with ropes holding it down stood over the open grave. There was a mound of fresh earth close to where we all stood, no chairs. The huge, dull, metal casket was suspended over the hole and artificial grass carelessly placed could not hide the grave of Jack's boyhood friend, Sebastian Sampas, next to the open crypt.

Where was Neal buried? And Joan? When I had been in Albany in the 1950s, I had called Joan's mother and asked where her grave was. Well, her mother never answered me and hung up! My, I was upset. I kept thinking of Jack saying, "Life slips away, as does the time of day."

When I saw all of these people—journalists, photographers, followers—I was truly surprised that so many knew Jack.

Where I'm from, Grosse Pointe, Michigan, you are surrounded by the "me" society. I mean, no one ever heard of or gave a damn about Jack Kerouac, and so I hadn't heard much about him either. If someone had heard of him it was his "beatnik" attributes: booze, broads, bums and pot. They were all there; people running, taking pictures, speaking into tape recorders in a dozen languages. They reminded me of scurrying squirrels. A priest stood nearby and I could feel he was saddened by the whole thing, as were several Greek women. Stella said that Jack's mother was too sick to make the trip from Florida.

Jack used to tell me how all the old women of Lowell would talk to one another over their picket fences and complain about how rotten their husbands were. Then, after they died, the same men became saints to these women. But then I thought, didn't Jack do the same thing with his brother and father, Gerard and Leo? Or did his mother make him feel guilty because he was alive instead of his saintly brother Gerard? Leo was much different than Jack had described. To me anyway, he was a tyrant and a bully. I didn't like him and was even afraid of him, to say the least. I always thought Jack's mother was a saint for putting up with him. I visited their flat in Ozone Park on Long Island often. Jack and I lived there for two weeks after we were married. Leo never mellowed down. It was easy to figure why Jack liked his mother and sister, Nin (short for Caroline), so much. Actually, his mother Gabe was the only one you could communicate with. Now that I am older, I can see that Gabe and Leo never should have stayed married. Jack had called me when Leo died. He was so upset, and I blasted him for being a hypocrite. I have since realized, reading his books and analyzing memories, that when someone dies your mind doesn't remember how that person really was, you only remember the good times. Jack had told me his father was a lot of fun when he was very young.

Suddenly Allen was standing before me, taking my hand and leading me into the open tent where we stood beside the casket. He was chanting a mantra and gave me a red rose and held one himself. He threw his on the casket and then waited for me to throw mine. I did, then turned and walked away. Tony Sampas took hold of my arm and we—Dee, Sister and I—made our way back to the car, leaving Jack in his casket behind us. Tony drove us to the Sampas's home. It was small and very clean—no carpeting, with beautiful Oriental throw rugs covering the shiny varnished floors. There was comfortable furniture and a huge dining room table that held an incredible feast of home cooked Greek food. All those Greek ladies were serving, cooking and bustling around this wonderful table. I was taken to a room where I was again introduced to Stella and her sister.

After a large swallow of scotch and soda, I felt much better and more at ease in the awkward situation. Everyone seemed friendly under the circumstances. Only a few, other than the Sampases, knew who I was. Stella told my sister how happy she was to have received her letter when Jack's book, *Vanity of Duluoz*, was published. Of course, the reason for Sister's letter was to tell Jack that she didn't like what he had written about me. *Vanity* was essentially Jack's autobiography, and aside from his accounts of my sister and me, he wrote about my mother, father and grandmother as well. After he read the letter, Jack called me and denied everything, I think tongue in cheek. It was just his sense of humor.

Tony came over to take me around the table and explain the different Greek foods to me. He handed me a plate, but what I needed was another scotch, so Tony was kind enough to go into the kitchen with me to get one. Their kitchen was medium sized with a sort of breakfast nook off it. Near the back door was another small room, a butler's pantry or a place to store pots and pans and dishes. We had one in our house in Asbury Park, but our pantry never saw a butler and I don't think theirs had either. Tony said, "This is where Sammy (Sebastian) and Jack spent most of their youth." And I could certainly see why.

I went back to sit and talk with Stella and sample some of that marvelous food. As I ate, Stella mentioned how she wished she had known me better and that she should have insisted I come to St. Petersburg, as Jack had so much wanted. Being terribly jealous of the other women in his life, she was sorry we didn't follow through.

Allen was nowhere to be found, so I asked Tony if he had seen him or the others. He said they were all upstairs. In the confusion at the gravesite, I had given Allen some old snapshots of all of us at Columbia University and I was getting nervous about them, and rightfully so. When I got them back, my photo of Jack and Lucien Carr at Columbia's fountain was missing. Unfortunately, I didn't notice until I was back in Michigan, but I have seen it published in several books since that time.

There were a lot of relatives, both Kerouacs and Sampases, milling around the house. I didn't know any of them. Jack's sister had died of a heart attack in 1966. At the time, Jack told me that she had died of a broken heart. Nin was a very sentimental, religious person who had married a man named Paul Blake. She was very much in love with him. Paul was Nin's

Jack Kerouac and Lucien Carr, Columbia University fountain, *ca.* 1943.

second husband. She had first married a boy from Lowell right after graduating from high school. I think love, real love, only comes once to the Kerouacs. That is why Jack and I never lost track of one another through all those years. Anyway, none of the Blakes were at the funeral. Nin's only child, Paul Blake, Jr., I knew. He was close to Jack, but he wasn't there either.

At that point I had come to the end of my ball of string and felt it was time to start heading back to my sister's house. Allen with his entourage, Orlovsky, Corso and some others, came down the narrow wooden stairs and handed me the envelope containing my photographs. Then he kissed me again. We both strongly felt the tragedy and the lost part of ourselves that now rested in his "Galloway" grave.*

As we drove back to Framingham, Dee asked me how Jack and I had met. Everything became very clear in my mind, and telling her the story of our first meeting and how we fell in love became a catharsis.

---

* Galloway was the fictitious name that Kerouac gave to his hometown.

chapter 2
. . .

I was born in Detroit, healthy and almost wealthy, on September 20, 1922. I say wealthy but it was my grandparents who had the money, and the more my life centered around theirs, the more lucrative was my life. I hated those strings and developed independent ways of thinking early on.

When I was young I was overactive and developed the habit of rejecting food; it took too much time. I also learned that the accessories of my life brought me the boys I wanted. It began with my first bicycles. I attracted the best boys with my elegant bikes, and many gorgeous fellows would jump onto my irresistible wheels.

My mother, Charlotte Maire, was one of nine children. Grandfather Maire was a self-made man, a pillar of Grosse Pointe society and a distinguished ophthalmologist. He maintained the Oak Ridge Farm in Dexter, Michigan, where I once

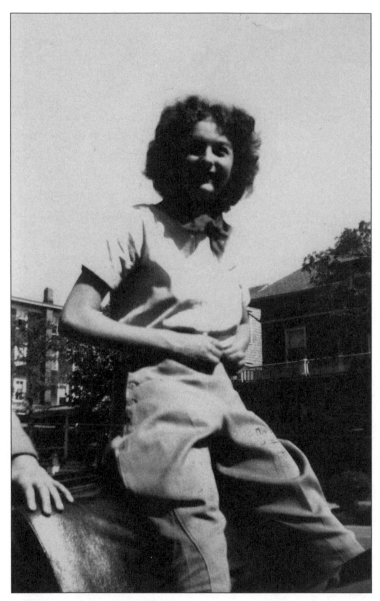

Edie Parker in Grosse Pointe, Michigan.

took Jack. I had always liked visiting the Dexter farm where I became fond of the small farm-town church and sang in the choir. My grandfather had been a gentleman farmer and raised prize bulls, pigs, cattle and sheep.

In spite of being born on opposite ends of the economic spectrum, there were many similarities between my life and Jack's. We were both born in 1922. Jack was seven months older than me, having been born on March 12 in Lowell, Massachusetts. My mother was in labor for over eight hours before I was born, Jack's mother for four. I was the first child and Jack was his mother's third. Both of us were fat babies.

I was born in my parent's house on Harding Avenue. It was a dark, somber brick building with stone pillars and steps, a carpeted staircase and dim electric lighting. As a child I would often scamper about on my hands and knees, acting like a dog. (I did this until I was over ten, and as I got older I fancied myself a horse, prancing and neighing.) The downstairs neighbor told my mother that all my noise was driving her to distraction.

My father was Walter Milton Parker, a handsome Manhattan sophisticate, six feet two inches tall, blue eyes, thick black wavy hair and a Charlie Chaplin mustache. I always thought he looked like Clark Gable, and so did he. He bought his clothes from all the best men's shops in New York, Brooks Brothers and Abercrombie and Fitch. Father drove the latest model Packards and Mercurys, always choosing white. He was seen as a likable eccentric, a good time Charlie, amiable, unaffected by pretense, yet perfectly aware of his station in life. He was an adventurer but would stray only so far, and he was generally loved for these qualities. How much like him I became!

My mother first met my father on a golf course in the Adirondacks in the early 1920s. Charlotte was one foot shorter than Walter and very attractive herself. She had once been a model for the Packard automobile company. Such modeling was very daring for a well brought up society girl in those days. It was looked on as scandalous by her parents. Originally my mother had married Wilfred Gordon, but he died seven months after their wedding in the great influenza epidemic of 1918. That early tragedy had a silver lining. Wilfred had owned a chain of shoe stores, Gordon's Ground Gripper Shoes, that left my mother financially independent. Widowed at age twenty, Charlotte returned to her parents' house in Grosse Pointe Park.

For his part, my father was a playboy who lived entirely for boats and women. My mother could tolerate his boats but not his infidelities. His yacht, "The Cigarette," was his pride and joy. He even named his dinghy, "The Butt," as a joke. The boat was thirty-eight feet long and twelve feet wide, long and slender, which inspired her name. There was a cabin, galley and two double bunk beds. Jack and I made love many times on those bunk beds underneath red Hudson Bay blankets, much of which he described in *Vanity of Duluoz*. It was a gallant ship, moving swiftly across the calm summer lakes, but not very sturdy when the lake threw a stormy tantrum. I spent hundreds of hours as a child on my father's boat, usually working for five dollars a week scraping the barnacles off the hull, polishing the brass and swabbing the deck. I didn't enjoy the work, but I loved the boat, life on the water and the yacht club where the boat was moored.

We would dive off the boat into the lake, arms outstretched

to a perfect point, back arched, legs straight together, toes pointed. I felt more like a dolphin than a person. I dove as deep as I dared, then kicked to go even deeper, my breath in bubbles tickling my nose. Finally I'd come back to the surface, breathless, and suck in the cool, clean lake air. Then I would return to the varnished deck of the Cigarette and stretch out on the bow.

I used to lie in bed with Jack and tell him how much I loved to swim in the fresh water of the lake, or wade in the surf on the Atlantic coast. At my grandmother's house in Asbury Park, New Jersey, I became an expert body surfer. Jack would tell me about his running, jumping and twisting maneuvers in football games. We both loved what our bodies could do, together in love and apart in sports. Jack could not swim well, nor ride horses, both of which I had mastered, but I was not skilled in contact sports in which he excelled. We complemented each other.

My mother's parents hated my father intensely and my father returned their sentiments. He resisted their attempts to interfere in our family life with their pious attitudes. He was not one to judge others and would not tolerate being judged. Grandfather Maire did not approve of drinking or idleness, and a man who was not busy working was not worth his salt to him. All that created a conflict for my mother, who was very loyal. She could not go against her family, despite her marriage to my father, and both men were too stubborn to meet halfway. My father could have easily become an executive in one of the companies that the Maires controlled but he shunned any such role. He was furious that my mother maintained her devotion to her family, but she was much more a Maire than a

Parker. So the marriage lasted only a short while, and when it was discovered that he was having an affair with my mother's cousin Ethel, it was the last straw.

My parents separated when I was eight years old while we were living on Lakepointe Drive in Grosse Pointe Park. My mother's maternal instincts were too great for my father. She would call home from parties continually to ask the maid about my sister and me. She was never at ease when she was away from her children.

At the time of her divorce my mother was running the last of the Ground Gripper shoe stores. My father had almost brought the company to bankruptcy. Mother had inherited twelve or thirteen outlets, but my father had squandered most of the assets until there was only the downtown Detroit store left.

Mother kept the Parker name until she remarried seventeen years later. In all that time she never invited another man into our house until we were fully grown. She was overprotective in the extreme, a quality which both Jack's mother and mine had in common. My father was exactly the opposite, he was anything but a homebody. He spent much of his time with the more promiscuous ladies of Grosse Pointe society and had many girlfriends. My sister and I were always permitted to visit our father, who divided his time between his yacht and his mother's homes in New York and Asbury Park. He eventually remarried, and as a result we lost any possibility of inheritance from the Parker side of the family.

My father's *bon vivant* lifestyle opened a completely different world to me, unlike the proper, cloistered existence of my mother's home. As a child I was perfectly aware of a more carefree, fun-loving, roaring-twenties side to life. My father would visit us often, taking my sister and me to the circus, a movie, or the yacht club to swim. Once he gave me a huge swimming party there. My father loved us dearly and was always joyful when we were with him. I was torn apart by his conflict with my mother; children always are. My mother's worst criticism of me in my rebellious years was that I "was just like my father!" It always stung to the quick, as much as I loved him.

My sister Charlotte was born three years after me. We moved from Harding Street to a duplex on Marquette across from the beautifully sculptured building of the Detroit Water Works, which we called "Willy Kerr Winks" for some reason. From this house I could visit Belle Isle across the river, which became our family's playground. It was a great place for a kid to explore and discover a blade of grass, a fallen leaf and the world around her.

My earliest childhood was the best time of my family life. Mom and Dad were still very much in love. My mother had the family she always wanted and Walter seemed to be a good father, which made all of us happy. Mother worked every day at the store and father increasingly spent his time aboard the Cigarette, chumming with his drinking and sailing buddies.

The Parker's summer home was at 312 Sixth Avenue in North Asbury Park, about fifty miles south of New York City. My grandparents had spent their summers there since even before my father was born. The house was two blocks from the ocean and had huge, wraparound porches both upstairs and down. That house was the greatest joy of my childhood with its wooden swing and abundant garden. The garden, with its innumerable variety of plants, luscious colors and scents, encouraged my already strong love of nature and horticulture.

In addition to plants, I have always loved animals. In fact, no house of mine has ever been without a dog. Although Jack preferred cats, we had both in our New York City apartments. My grandmother's dog Rex, a German Shepherd, was the dog I walked as a developing teenager in Asbury Park and New York. My current sweet thing, a large Belgian sheepdog named Samantha, keeps me company as I write this memoir. She is well into her old age but we still enjoy our daily walks through the garden and on the streets.

I was named after my grandmother, Frankie Edith Parker. She lived with my grandfather until he died in 1942 in a large four-bedroom apartment on the Upper West Side of Manhattan, very close to Columbia University. My grandfather, Walter Mackay Parker, spent most of his time at the New York Athletic Club and the New York Engineers Club. He was a very formal man and always signed his letters to me as "W.M. Parker" instead of granddad. Once when he gave a speech at the Detroit Athletic Club he pulled out his handkerchief to blow his nose, only to discover that it was a pair of my silk panties I had slipped into his pocket as a joke. The crowd roared and he told my mother it was the only speech he had ever given that had gotten a laugh. He was involved in making steel for shipyards, a legacy from the Mackay side of the family. Almost from the beginning my life was divided between Grosse Pointe, Asbury Park and New York. I considered all three to be my home without any distinction; none was second to the other.

In this golden time of my youth I knew nothing of poverty, only privilege and prosperity. It was a world of crimson sunsets that flooded the western horizon at dusk as my father's boat rocked gently on the lake. I had a horse that grazed calmly in the dewy pastures on our farm in Dexter and in the spring I rode across the plowed fields on his back. Yet, for all its expansiveness, my world was also restricted, enclosed and private. As I grew older, I realized that my freedom was only relative. The outside world was not open to me, but forbidden territory. I was trapped inside one green ghetto after another. These were ghettos of sculptured lawns and leaded glass windows; ghettos of "Private: Do Not Enter" signs; ghettos of gold leaf, polished brass and oak paneled rooms in country clubs and yacht clubs. All were ghettos; ghettos of gluttony and inebriation; ghettos bejeweled and bequeathed from generation to generation, the blood running thinner, the boredom and the passivity growing. My only escape from this gilded cage was to be found in my friends, a growing circle of people who made my life interesting.

I was a playful, overactive child, a gregarious high-energy adventurer always seeking to escape the boundaries of prudent parental guidance. Our maid had to wrestle me into the bathtub after my long days in the gardens and playfields. Usually I was dirty from playing games like "king of the mountain." One time I socked a little boy off the mountain and he ran home and told his father that Frankie had hit him. When his father appeared with the little boy with his black eye at our doorstep to complain to my father, he was embarrassed to find that "Frankie" was a little girl in a silk dress.

As a student, I also gave the teachers trouble. In elementary school I demanded my freedom and became an expert at playing hooky. I found most of the required subjects dull. I loved to be a tomboy and was more fond of playing with the boys than with the other girls. This caused concern from my mother, but when my father was around he'd just laugh and tell my mother to let me have some fun.

chapter 3

. . .

At seventeen I had become restless and dreamed of pursuing a career in art in the big city—New York. I grew to hate high school and felt out of place among the industrial automotive scions of Detroit. I wanted to be an artist and live a completely independent bohemian life. After a good deal of begging on my part and with the support of my grandmother, my mother finally relented and gave me permission to take my shot at living in New York with my grandmother. Of course, my mind was racing far ahead of my mother's and grandmother's. My imagination saw me in my own apartment in Manhattan, and then maybe in Paris living and painting on the Left Bank—a true artist in every crazy way.

It was right after Halloween when I moved into my grandmother's apartment on Morningside Heights. I always felt welcome there. Jessie and Ward, the "do everything" maintenance men, grinned as they opened the front doors for me. Ward took my bags up in the large cage elevator while Jessie parked the car a block away on Morningside Drive.

My father drove me into the city from Asbury Park, where he and I greeted grandmother. He called her "Mother," I called her "Gram," Grandpa called her "the Madam," and everyone else called her "Aunt Frank."

I was given a room the size of a cubbyhole with one window that looked out onto a brick wall no more than two feet away from the glass panes that hadn't been cleaned in years. I felt like I was living in a doghouse. Even though it was cold outside, the room was warm. I had a dresser, too large for the tiny room, where I could put my clothes. In order to open the closet door you had to first close the bedroom door. So there I was in New York, already feeling like a cramped New Yorker.

I wanted to go out and get the newspapers to study the want ads for a job, and I decided to cut through the Columbia University campus just across the street. I knew all of the boys' eyes were on me as I strolled past in my swinging brown suede skirt and saddle shoes. At 116th Street and Broadway, I don't know if it is still there, was a corner drug store. I went in and picked up all the papers that had want ads in them—the *New York Herald*, the *New York Times* and the *New York Journal*—and then headed home to begin the search. Unfortunately, there weren't many "Help Wanted Female" ads, so I had to wait for the larger Sunday papers.

Shortly after moving into Gram's apartment I met Henri Edouard Cru. He and his mother, a French professor at Barnard, happened to live in the same apartment house. Henri's mother was divorced from his father, Albert. Henri was tall—six feet, one inch—with black hair, black eyes and a smooth, tanned complexion. He had a certain charm in his words and spoke French fluently. All of this made him quite attractive to women, and I certainly was not opposed to men, so Henri and I began seeing each other.

Henri had attended Horace Mann Prep School for a while before he was expelled for selling condoms and switchblade knives to his classmates. He had decided to join the merchant marine, and he was studying to get his seaman's papers as an electrician at the Sheepshead Bay training station in Brooklyn when I met him.

One evening Henri came by at about five o'clock for a date and sat and talked with Dad and Gram. He never really said very much and I think that's why Gram liked him. He just looked good and smelled even better. Henri and I took the subway downtown to Columbus Circle and then walked east along Central Park South as far as the Plaza Hotel. There we sat in the main dining room where I ordered coffee for myself, while Henri had a drink.

We talked about my half-brother Bill, who was planning to come to New York for a visit when he got leave from boot camp before being assigned to duty. He had been a British soldier at Dunkirk before he received citizenship in this country and enlisted in the American army. Before long Henri began talking of marriage, but I could only think about all the marriages I knew. It seemed that only the women were bound in marriage; the men weren't. So I gave him a 'What, are you crazy?' look. He said, "Let's get a room here for the night. We'll have dinner sent up and listen to the music being piped up from the ballroom." I thought it all sounded very romantic

Henri Cru, 1944.

and expensive; it was going to cost him at least thirty-five bucks for the room. I imagined what it would be like to spend the night at the Plaza with handsome Henri, but I declined his offer. He smiled, then paid the tab.

We got up and strolled down the hall to the Oak Room, stopping to look in the various display cases that were filled with an assortment of items for sale. I told Henri that the department stores were looking for female models and that I was going to apply the next morning. Henri believed it was a tremendous idea and encouraged me to do so. He certainly enjoyed having a beautiful woman on his arm, as well as a refined one. Henri said he had dated many models from the Powers School. Although I liked clothes well enough, I wasn't completely convinced that the job would be right for me. I had other things on my mind.

We stood at the entrance to the Oak Room, watching as we waited for a table. It was very crowded with celebrities at the time. Walter Winchell sat at the bar talking—his unmistakable voice rising above the others. He was interviewing Betty Grable for a live radio broadcast. The maître'd seemed to be impressed by Henri's uniform; I think he thought Henri must have been some Admiral he didn't recognize. As a result, we wound up with a great table with an excellent view of everything that was going on around us. Barbara Stanwyck sat two tables away. We glanced back and forth at one another. I always thought that we looked very much alike, and perhaps she did, too.

Our salads came and were delicious, but I found that Henri's conversation often turned into lectures on what to do, when and how to do it and whom to do it with. He was a character right out of a Damon Runyon novel and it was hard to believe that he was schooled in Paris. Henri droned on, "I think that with Hitler gobbling up every country he can, war will surely reach the United States before long. I was talking to my friend, Jack Kerouac, the other day and he said that the Communists in Spain should get more support fighting the Nazis. That would keep the war over there."

"How is Jack . . . what's he up to?" I asked Henri. I recalled Henri and I having bumped into him briefly once before.

"He's playing football at Columbia and hating every minute of it," he answered.

"That's funny, I thought he was on a football scholarship," I replied. Henri told me, "He doesn't like the way they play. It's a clique. And the coach, Lou Little, thinks he's a little smartass Canuck, see, which is preposterous, because Jack's not even from Canada. He's from Lowell. Jack's father stuck his nose in the whole mess of Jack's contract and told Little off, saying he hated 'kikes' and what could he and Jack expect from a bunch of them? Well, Jack was mortified and now he's on Little's shit list. He makes Jack scrimmage for hours and then only puts him in at the very end of the game."

"Gee, that's too bad," I said.

The Oak Room was getting more crowded by the minute, so Henri and I didn't linger over coffee. We walked through the lobby, stopping to admire the gorgeous jewelry once again before we made our way out of the Plaza's main entrance to the fountain directly across the street. Henri offered to take me on a hansom cab ride, but it was too cold for me. Instead, we walked down Fifth Avenue, browsing the big windows of the most elegant shops in the world. Christmas was not far off and the city had begun to take on the beauty and aura of the season. Henri suggested we walk down to Rockefeller Center to have a hot chocolate and watch the ice skaters, so we did just that. The Christmas music and the rhythm of the skating was like a waltz, with lots of twirling skirts and ruffled petticoats exposed. There were a few short skirts, but I've found the way to a man is not to let him see all, even if his mind imagines that he has.

"Let's take in a movie," Henri said, "I hear that Hemingway's *Farewell to Arms* is playing on Forty-Second Street." We grabbed a cab and when we arrived, there was a line. Still, we had no problem getting in. It was a tremendous film about ambulance drivers saving the lives of handsome brave men. By the end of the film I had made a promise to myself to join the Red Cross Ambulance Corps.

We took the crowded express subway home. The ride from 42nd Street to 116th Street was only ten minutes and its speed took your breath away. When we came up to the street at the Broadway stop, the West End Bar was right there. At that point, it was about one in the morning, and we went inside for a drink. The place was jumping. A lot of Henri's Horace Mann buddies were sitting together in a booth. He waved to them as he looked for a place for us to sit down. Once we were seated, Henri excused himself and went over to talk with his former classmates. I was surprised to see an old friend of mine from Asbury Park, Bill Sufton. He came over and said he didn't know I was from New York City and I explained to him that I wasn't. Right away he asked me for my phone number. He said he was a member of the Columbia football team and then asked me to go to their prom with him. I told him to call or come by and he said he would just as Henri came back to the table. After some small talk, Sufton split. I told Henri that I knew him from the beach at Asbury Park where he was a lifeguard. Henri was pissed off, so I told him that I liked dark-haired men better. Sufton was a big, burly, blond guy. Henri gave me a half grin, half smirk, from the side of his mouth. He was so damn sure of himself and his fatal charms that it would grind me sometimes. You know the type. After a beer we walked home.

Henri was off for the weekend and was staying at his mother's upstairs. Jessie took us up in the elevator, letting me off on the second floor. When I got to the door I turned the lighted bell on, not wanting to wake Grandpa. The bell would have startled Rex, their dog, into barking. After a few minutes Gram noticed the light and let me in. For my grandparents it was very late, but they always felt secure knowing I was with Henri.

The next morning I slept in. At about 9:00 A.M., I heard Ward come to take Rex for his walk. He said the weather was bad, so I rolled over and went back to sleep. I woke later with a start, remembering that I wanted to go to the Red Cross that day to see about joining. I got up, dressed, and went down to the tearoom for coffee and breakfast. There, I ran into Stewart Miller and joined him. Stewart also lived in the building with his mother. He was excited about a face cream he had just invented and gave me a jar to try out. "Very nice," I commented. He asked me if I would consider modeling for his line of cosmetics, which sounded very interesting to me. "Can I meet you here for tea this afternoon and we'll talk some more?" I asked. "Great," Stew said.

Off I went on the bus downtown to the Red Cross, located in what was once the Vanderbilt Mansion. When I arrived I walked through a huge, ornate iron gate that stood at the foot of a semi-circular stone drive. The property was enclosed by a tall iron fence and there were enormous Red Cross flags everywhere. Unfortunately, the inside was not quite as impressive. There was a big, old wooden desk in the foyer and people in Red Cross uniforms milling around it. One handed me a form to fill out. It wasn't as difficult as I had anticipated. My only medical experience was having worked for my Uncle Ed, a doctor, in his office on Saturdays. No one questioned me any further. I signed the necessary papers and was told that I could start that Monday at 9 A.M., when I would be sworn in.

Monday morning came and I was there at 9 A.M. sharp. There were only two other recruits. We struck up a conversation, and one of the girls said she hadn't known it was a non-paying position and wondered what she would do to make a living. Where was she from that she didn't know the Red Cross is volunteer? We stood around drinking coffee and I eyed the uniforms, which I could just envision myself wearing.

chapter 4
. . .

The modeling job Stewart had spoken of seemed the perfect
solution to how I could support myself and volunteer, too. I
went back to the apartment and found Stewart waiting for me.
We went to have tea and he told me he had arranged for me
to have a photo session, right then, with a photographer by the
name of Andre Shaub. His studio was on Broadway, close to
Columbia, right above one of the old automat type restaurants
called Chock Full O'Nuts. We finished our tea and walked
through Columbia's campus to Broadway. It was cold as the
winds whistled across 116th Street from the Hudson River.
Shaub's studio reminded me of something out of a Sam Spade
novel. A gum snapping, hard blond receptionist led us back to
meet Shaub. He was a man of about forty, dark and swarthy.
He reminds me now of Charles Bronson. He spoke with a
thick accent as he greeted me, kissing my hand, then lightly

clicking his heels. He shook Stewart's hand and greeted Stewart's mother, who was with us. I thought, "Oh brother! What I won't do for money."

He scrutinized me thoroughly and remarked to Stew that I looked like I would be a good model—that I had all the attributes. He asked if I felt I was photogenic and whether I had any experience at this. I told him that my grandmother had been taking pictures and painting oil portraits of me since I was a tot. Gram had been doing oils from photographs since the early 1900s, and in fact was one of the first to do so.

Shaub took us into a large studio filled with lights hanging all over the room. There were two big wooden armchairs draped with exotic material, a rocker and a faded blue velvet fainting couch. He asked me to sit on the rocker with my legs over the arms, a pillow for my back and one under my legs. He reached over and took the ribbons from my hair, causing it to tumble down in thick ringlets. That seemed to please him. He started shooting in rapid succession as I changed the position of my head. Then he caught me off guard by asking what I thought of posing with less clothes on. "You're an art student, aren't you? You should be accustomed to nudity." I didn't want him or the Millers to think that I was unsophisticated, so I told him we could discuss it later after he paid me and after I saw how these shots turned out.

Stewart stayed behind to speak with Shaub while his mother and I made our way back home. I was just in time to get a phone call from my brother Bill, who said he would be coming in from North Carolina in time for Thanksgiving. Apparently he had been having trouble with his stomach, and the army had granted him ten days sick leave in order to send

Head shots of Edie Parker by Andre Shaub.

him to Red Bank, New Jersey, for treatment. I hung up smiling, knowing he would arrive in just a couple of days.

I went upstairs to find out what plans Gram had for dinner, but as usual, she had eaten her main meal at noon and had tea at four. I would have to fend for myself. Henri was coming by at seven and I hoped we might go to the Kingsley Arms for dinner.

Henri had a special knock he used so I always knew that it was him. I answered the door and he swept in—tall, handsome, smelling good and wearing his uniform. He went into the living room and sat down next to Gram. "The weather looks pretty bad out there," I said, "I thought we could go to the Kingsley Arms." "Great idea," Henri replied.

Off we went, both hungry. It was terrible walking uphill to the Kingsley Arms, a tall apartment house with an elegant restaurant on the roof top. The elevator doors opened and we stepped out into the restaurant foyer where there was a bench, surrounded by large plants, that separated the waiting area from the rest of the restaurant. The maitre'd seated us at a table for two next to the window. It was like sitting in a glass up among the clouds. The tablecloths were gold and matched the carpets. Mirrors and crystal were everywhere with large white and gold chrysanthemums strategically placed about the room. There was even a big, light blue "C.U." for Columbia University, woven into the center of the carpet—all very posh.

Henri ordered a bottle of red wine, while a little man in a red double-breasted uniform with gold buttons and braid stood at the table holding a menu board for us. I remarked to Henri that this guy's uniform could give his a run for its money, but Henri ignored me. Just then, Henri's father walked in. Albert Louis Cru was chairman of the French department at Teacher's College, Columbia University. In addition, he was a well-respected editor and translator of French literature. One of the books he edited, *Sans Famille* by Hector Malot, was dedicated to Henri. Later Jack told me he was quite impressed by Mr. Cru, since he always wanted to be considered a great French writer himself. *Sans Famille* dealt with the travels of a boy named Remi who was searching for his mother and brother. Remi Boncoeur (good hearted) would later become Henri's name in Jack's *On the Road*.

Mr. Cru was dressed in formal wear, as were his companions. Henri said they were on their way to the opera. We just waved to them because Henri said he was with some important people from the prep school—a writer and poet named Kenneth Rexroth. "That reminds me," Henri said, "I want you to meet a friend of mine from Horace Mann, Jack Kerouac, we met on the Mann football team. He was a tremendous player, but he suffered a broken leg. Remember you met him last fall, he was on crutches?"

"Oh yeah, I remember—why?" I asked.

"Well, he is a great writer and poet himself, and I thought maybe he could tell you about the art teachers at Columbia. You know, which is best, which classes you should take next spring . . . just a thought," he shrugged his shoulders. "We'll have lunch next Monday at Lou's Deli if that sounds good? I won't have to be back to Sheepshead Bay until mess, which is around four." "Sounds good to me," I said.

"Now Edith," Henri said as he patted my hand, "Jack is my number one pal from Horace Mann. He helped me with a lot of my schoolwork. He was there on a football scholarship, but he was a real genius, too. When they passed out brains, he got in line twice, know what I mean?"

We finished our meal and Henri signaled for the waiter and ordered a cognac while I had crème de menthe. With it our waiter brought us a plate of sweets; cookies, mints and Turkish candies. Then Henri began to talk about us going to bed. That was something I didn't go for, as it was like making an appointment with the dentist. I felt it should just happen spontaneously, but some guys just never seem to learn. He said we could use his dad's apartment while he was at the opera. I guess he just assumed I would be anxious to go with him, but I didn't respond. That made Henri angry, and his silence seemed an eternity. It was then that he laid that bullshit line on me, "What is it . . . you don't love me enough?" Still I didn't answer. "Well, I guess not," Henri said. He paid the bill, took me by the elbow and purposefully escorted me home. I was in my own bed by ten o'clock.

The wind from the storm had died down a bit, but the rain and snow continued to fall. I lay there crying, unable to understand why I had rejected Henri's advances. He was everything a girl could want and certainly better than anyone I had known back in Grosse Pointe. Henri even had marriage on his mind, but maybe that was it, he was too serious. I finally fell asleep with my mind spinning and my body exhausted.

On Sunday morning Gram, Grandpa and I went down to the tearoom for breakfast. Gram was making her Thanksgiving plans, brother Bill and Dad would be coming. Grandpa was not real big on the idea but kept it to himself; he never said boo. By then I was beginning to realize that living with old people wasn't much fun. I told them that I didn't plan to stay with them for very long and that I hoped to be accepted as an ambulance driver for the Red Cross. Grandpa seemed only mildly impressed. Mainly he wanted to know what my school plans were and what I intended to do for money. I told him that I had heard that Columbia took a certain number of "special" students who didn't have their high school diplomas but were able to pass the entrance exams. I felt that if I could get in to study art, I could look for a part-time job later. I didn't mention my dream of having my own apartment. There was a chance, I thought, that I might get an overseas assignment with the Red Cross, so I didn't see any point in upsetting them. We had just finished our breakfast and were heading out when Henri came in with his mother and sister, Yvonne. We all exchanged pleasantries and Henri said to me, "I'll see you later."

Since I had to take Rex out for his Sunday walk, I went ahead of Gram and Grandpa. It was a crisp, refreshing blue-sky day, so Rex and I went down to Riverside Park. The sun felt warm on my face. We sat at Grant's Tomb, Gram's favorite spot because she had something to do with raising the money to build it. While I sat I dreamed about the romance of going to France, meeting a wonderful man, marrying him and settling in Paris. I thought of the photographer, Shaub, and how I didn't like him; he was so obvious and grabby. And I thought of Henri, who was so handsome and wanted me to marry him. We could easily live in New York or Paris, but surprisingly Henri had no interest in Paris after having gone to school there. His mom and dad were so highly educated that all he ever wanted was to be a merchant seaman and catch a good ship. Then I thought of an old boyfriend, Tooie Snyder, back in Grosse Pointe. He didn't have any plans of going anywhere either.

As Rex and I walked back you could hear the student choir singing inside Riverside Church. Their voices floated out through the huge, beautiful stained glass windows. It was all very inspiring. As we walked down the hill toward 116th Street, we passed a striking man in a wheelchair being pushed uphill in the opposite direction by Henri's friend, Jack Kerouac. (Only later did I learn that the man in the wheelchair was none other than Cole Porter.) "Hi," I said to Jack, who just nodded. Rex and I kept going, not giving them another thought or a glance back.

When I got back to our building, Henri was waiting for me in the lobby. I had to laugh, for he was sitting on a "King Arthur" armchair flanked by two huge, yellow chrysanthemums. "Well, well . . . if it isn't King Arthur," I joked. Henri failed to see the humor. He usually didn't think anything was quite as amusing as his own jokes; it must have been his French schooling.

I went upstairs to put Rex away and Gram asked what I was up to. "Henri and I are going over to the church to listen to the Julliard Choir sing," I told her. Henri, as I recall, was never very affectionate. Sure, he talked of love and making love, but he would never hold hands or hug or show any signs of affection in public. He kept talking about the Red Cross, telling me it was hard work and warning me that it would not be fun. "Are you certain you want to do this Edith?" he asked. "Henri, you sound like my father, not my boyfriend. Don't you think I can make up my own mind?" I responded.

When we got to the church we found seats in the rear as the performance had already begun. The choir was humming "White Christmas" and it couldn't have sounded more glorious. I looked around and noticed Jack sitting in a pew next to Mr. Porter's wheelchair in the aisle. The music, the singing and the whole atmosphere made for a very moving evening. When the performance ended Henri left to speak with someone he knew. There were a lot of people and it didn't take long for me to lose track of Henri, so I decided to walk back to the Fairmont alone and sit in the King Arthur chair to wait for him. Eventually he showed up and told me that we were to have lunch with Jack at the deli down the street. "Lou's, you know the one? Across from the dorms, next to the Chinese laundry."

"When?" I asked. "Tomorrow, and please be sure to be on your best behavior."

I was the first to arrive. I was wearing a red plaid skirt that swung from side to side when I walked, a white pullover sweater with a waist length string of pearls tied in a low hanging knot, Spaulding saddle shoes and, of course, "Bobby" socks. I sat down at one of the little wire bistro tables with a round marble top and matching chairs. Once I got myself situated I thought about the time Henri had introduced Jack to me six months earlier on Amsterdam Avenue. It was very brief and I remember that Jack was on crutches from a football injury of some sort.

By now Jack had already graduated from Horace Mann and had gone on to Columbia. Henri, however, never graduated, but had succeeded in getting his seaman's papers after he was expelled. Then, in walked Jack. I recognized him immediately though he was no longer on crutches. He was wearing a navy blue sweater, a white shirt, open at the neck and loafers. My God, I thought, was he handsome. Jack put his books down on the table just as Henri arrived right behind him, beaming. Henri was wearing his officer's cap and uniform, which he had paid a tailor to convert from an ordinary suit. It was calculated to impress his father and chicks. Henri's conversation was amusing as always. "Now tell her what you've been writing and reading, Jack. Edith, isn't he something? Listen to how smart he is," and things like that. Poor Jack was so shy he needed someone like Henri to pry his mouth open. Jack's eyes were periwinkle blue and had a certain drowsiness about them. He had a lock of hair that always fell over his right eye and he would brush it back with four fingers up. Jack carried a comb for his cowlick—it was the scourge of his vanity. His voice was musical and hit all the keys. When he spoke, which was seldom, everyone would listen and he always enunciated his words perfectly. It was a great source of pride with him to have an incredibly large vocabulary. After we had fallen in love, Jack would teach me a new word every day. I still find them popping out of me, although half the time I can't recall what they mean. He was also an excellent speller. I became a great frustration to him because I couldn't spell worth a damn. I always believed that Jack's excellent command of English was supported by his first language, French. He often told me in our bedroom talks, that he thought first in French.

Jack Kerouac posing as a Gide character during the winter of 1944–45.

chapter 5
· · ·

That first day at the deli, we all ordered hot dogs. Now in
Michigan, we didn't have hotdogs and sauerkraut on a bun.
Combine that with my nervousness over being so taken by
Jack that before I knew it, I had eaten five hotdogs! Jack told
me later that after he saw me eat all those hotdogs, he fell in
love. The next day I received the most beautiful love letter from
Jack, written in what to me was a Shakespearean style. I was
hooked.

Everything was new to me. I had never been interested in
anything literary. If I read a book at all it was Thorn Smith or
Zane Gray. So I was eager to learn what I could from Jack, and
he was anxious to teach me. We approached our relationship
as teacher and student, all the time just wanting to be together.

Henri and I had been close and we had even had sex a few
times. He figured that we were committed, not necessarily to

marriage, but for me to be his steady girl and not to stray from him. We never discussed it and Henri simply said, "That is the way it is."

At lunch, Henri informed us that he would be shipping out soon and that he was leaving me in Jack's care until he returned. Well, he might as well have put an ice cream cone in my hand and told me not to eat it. From then on, Jack began showing up at my grandmother's apartment each day and then again in the evenings. My grandmother was deaf, so it was bad for her and good for us. Half the time she didn't even know that Jack was in the apartment. She was always in her bedroom and asleep by ten o'clock, so I could slip out with Jack and his Horace Mann buddy from London, Seymour Wyse, to go to Harlem and hit the jazz clubs. Seymour had an older brother Dave, who worked for a jazz magazine called *Downbeat,* so we always knew where the best musicians would be playing: Lester Young, Billie Holiday, Charlie Parker, Coleman Hawkins, Ben Webster, and so on. Minton's, at 117th and Lexington Avenue, became a favorite spot of ours. Many times I would not get home until early in the morning. Jack and I were together all the time and things were beginning to get very sticky.

We spent a lot of time at a hotel around the corner on 115th Street where Jack took a job on the switchboard after he quit the football team to be a writer. We spent a lot of happy hours in his little room there. I recall a small bed with a brown plaid spread, one large chair, a table, a lamp, a desk and a round green rug on the floor.

Both Jack and I were very bashful. We slept together for nearly eight months before we ever saw each other naked. He wore boxer shorts and I kept a sheet wrapped around me during our most intimate moments. If he heard a sound in the apartment he would quickly jump into his pants, which were always beside the bed. His skin was salty, his body odorless. When we made love, I'd get prickly heat from his wiry chest hair. In the morning he shaved with a gold razor that used very thick blades, which I remember were very hard to find. By 5:30 in the afternoon, he looked as if he hadn't shaved at all. Jack was fastidious about his teeth and used a combination of Pepsodent toothpaste and baking soda. He always carried his toothbrush in the breast pocket of his shirt. He never wore a watch, never wore a ring, and didn't like to wear socks.

After a while Jack's job at the hotel had run its course and he decided to join the merchant marine like Henri. He shipped out shortly thereafter. I took a job modeling and selling at Best & Co. on Fifth Avenue, but it wasn't long before I noticed that something was wrong. Things were happening to my body and I realized I was pregnant. Boy was I scared. Henri and Jack were both gone and I didn't know what to do, so I told my grandmother. One of her closest friends was a Dr. Martin who arranged for me to see an abortion doctor up in the Bronx on the Grand Concourse. I went there with my grandmother and he told us that I was about three months along. He recommended I wait a couple more months and then he could help me. During this time I received one "v-mail" letter from Jack and two from Henri. The problem was, all v-mail was censored and they could not reveal where they were, nor when they were going to return. I wrote to Jack's mother to see if she knew where Jack was, and received an answer. She said that she hadn't heard from Jack and was worried about the news of frequent U-boat attacks against merchant ships, but she was confident he was all right. His allotment checks were still coming, and had he been killed she knew the checks would stop immediately. That didn't keep her from reading the shipping news each day in search of word about his boat, though.

Two months later my grandmother and I went back to the doctor on a rainy Saturday afternoon. He put me on the examination table, placed a coarse white sheet over me, gave me two shots and then proceeded to force labor. After several hours of excruciating pain, it was over. It was a black-haired baby boy. Gram took me back in a cab and I immediately went to bed—spending the next five painful days there. During my convalescence Henri returned and came to see me, and I told him everything. He was so upset he could not speak and left the apartment. After a few hours, he came back. He sat by my side, took my hands in his and told me that it was all his fault. He said he would do right by my honor and marry me. When I told him that I thought the child was Jack's, he still insisted we marry, but I refused.

A short time later, Jack returned from sea. Henri and I met Jack at the West End Bar where we sat in a large dark booth, Jack and Henri opposite me. Henri told Jack what had happened. Jack was stunned and asked me if it were true. "Yes," I said. He then became furious. I never saw him get so angry, ever. I was glad that Henri kept talking, trying to calm him down. "Now Jack, what was this poor little lady to do? Both of us were gone. The child could have been either one of ours . . . a boy you know. But I want to make it up to her and I've been waiting for her to say yes and marry me. What do you think?"

Jack did not answer. "As you see, we've been waiting for you to return to get your reactions to this very serious matter." Jack banged his fist down hard on the table, challenging Henri to get up and fight, but then he left. Henri said, "There, there my dear, he'll storm around a while and then we'll get his answer later."

"How do you know?" I asked him. "He's a Frenchman, isn't he? Now drink your beer and we'll take a stroll. It's a nice balmy night."

Henri took me home early and I went straight to bed. I was really shaken and felt alone. My grandmother favored the wrong man—Henri. This love triangle was getting a bit tight and I knew I had to be careful.

It was about two o'clock in the morning when I heard a knock at the door. It was Jack. He was sweating and seemed a little drunk. He asked me, "Don't you know I love you?" "Well, yes . . . I guess so," I said. He came in and we talked for quite a while about what we were going to do about our feelings. In the end we decided to try to find an apartment and live together. The biggest obstacle would be to find rent money.

At the time a friend of mine, Joan Vollmer Adams, was attending Barnard. She had come to New York from Loudonville, a suburb of Albany where her father managed a manufacturing plant of some sort. Like me, she was eager to escape to the city and live her own, independent life. By the time I met her Joan was married to a soldier named Paul Adams, but he wasn't around very much. She thought it would be a great idea for me, Jack and her to share the expenses of an apartment. Since Joan had become my closest girlfriend, we both thought living together would be a lot of fun.

Joan Vollmer Adams on Morningside Heights, 1944.

chapter 6
. . .

Joan was getting Paul's allotment checks and a good healthy
allowance for attending Barnard. I was also getting an allowance
from my family in Detroit and in the spring would be starting
classes at Columbia. Jack agreed to help us look for an apartment, so the three of us started walking the streets around
Columbia in search of our new home. We didn't have much luck
at first, but we left Joan's name with several building supers since
she sounded the most respectable, with a "Mrs." in front of her
name. We were all planning to go home for Christmas, so it was
just as well if we didn't have to plunk down rent money right
away since we wouldn't even be in New York. Jack was going to
go to Boston and try to get into the Navy Air Corps with the
help of G.J., his old buddy from Lowell.

My father and my half-brother liked both Henri and Jack,
but my grandmother, maybe because of the abortion, disliked

Jack. That was the main reason I was anxious to move out of her apartment. While brother Bill was in New York we all went out a few times. His army stories were always exciting. Once, in London right after Dunkirk, he and a Scottish soldier paid $60 for a head of lettuce and sat down on the curb and ate it. Bill's uniform was also unusual, for he wore a green plaid highlander hat with ribbon streamers, wide leather straps that crossed his chest, medals and high leather boots with khaki pants tucked in. He was quite a sight in places like the West End Bar, and created a lot of attention. It was then that Jack and I met another writer by the name of John L. Fitzgerald.

Fitz, as we called him, was best friends with Duncan Purcell. In their group were Dicki Goebel, Bob Ritt, a boy named Jimmy and his girl Inez. Dicki was just five feet tall, gay, and walked with a limp, reminding us of a cricket. He worked on Wall Street as a secretary. Duncan and Fitz were both from Poughkeepsie, attended Columbia University and were complete opposites in appearance and personality. Fitz was blond, blue-eyed and taller than Jack. He was very sweet and adored by everyone. He became one of my best friends and also Jack's. Duncan, "Uncle Dunc" as we called him, was tall, large and silent. He spoke very little, but was very intelligent and basically a nice person. Our expanding group usually met at the West End for beer and dinner. The conversations were always stimulating, frequently about the war that crept into our world or all the new and exciting things that went on at school in New York. We never could get it all said, or begin to get it all done, but we tried.

Columbia was an all-boys school at the time, occupied by more and more of the navy's "90-day wonders." All of New

York seemed to be filled with soldiers, and nowhere more than on campus where most of the classes were filled with men training to be officers. Suddenly the West End had a lot more women hanging out there as a result. We became acquainted with many who would drift in and out, but Joan and I were the mainstays of our "Apartment Club." Many of the women we met had apartments around Columbia University. They were mostly Europeans, very exotic in appearance and language and they all had stories about the war and their escape from the bombs of Hitler. These women certainly had a much different outlook on life, love and the pursuit of happiness. They were a lot less moral than the women I had known—liberated you might better call it.

We finalized our plans to go home for Christmas. Jack would go to Lowell, Joan to Albany, Fitz and Uncle Dunc to Poughkeepsie, and I would return to Michigan for the holidays. Only Dicki, Seymour and his brother, who already lived in New York, would stay put.

With the country at war and all of us uncertain about our futures, we decided to have one last party before we left. We picked Dicki's apartment in Greenwich Village, and Dicki couldn't have been more thrilled. On our last Friday night we all met at the West End to go down together to Dicki's place. There were so many of us that we took up half a subway car. There was a singing group with us from Julliard, and we all joined in the fun. Seymour invited a fantastic piano player from Julliard who had been with us on some of our Harlem jazz escapades. Boy, could he play! Jack brought his bongos and Joan and I just sang.

Dicki's apartment was in an old brownstone on Washington Square. His building was unique—it was very narrow, four floors tall with one apartment on each floor and a small open cage elevator going up the middle of the building passing through each apartment. Every floor hung tapestries, oriental rugs, Venetian blinds or screens just outside the elevator to permit privacy when the elevator went by. Someone always made a provocative remark whenever they passed a floor since you could hear the passengers, but never see them.

Dicki knew everyone, and everyone was invited. We drank beer and wine, but the hard booze was mostly kept out of sight. There were so many people that we sat on the floor. The record player was the focal point and we sang and played along with the music—banging on pots, pans, bottles and whatever we could find to make sound.

Burl Ives, the famous folksinger, lived next door with his wife in his own brownstone. He dropped in with his banjo and we sang his "Shoo Fly" number. Jack and I later went to dinner at Ives' house for a small party. Katharine Hepburn lived around the corner on Fifth Avenue. Greenwich Village at that time was full of celebrities. We would see Humphrey Bogart on the street in the Village, or at our favorite little Italian restaurant called Minetta's on MacDougal Street.

That night Jack and I planned on ending our final evening together early. Dicki had been trying to encourage us to move to the Village, but Jack and I both agreed that the area around Columbia was our home. All the guests left early, going to different restaurants in small groups based on which restaurant or ethnic food they had a taste for. We did not have pizza parlors or plastic, short-order chain restaurants back then. Chinese or French cuisine was the cheapest. A favorite French place of ours served onion soup from a huge tureen which was placed in the middle of the table accompanied by all the French bread and real butter you could eat for only fifty cents. Most of the best spots were in the Village, far from touristy Times Square. Many of them would soon disappear, victims of the war and food rationing.

Minetta's was our choice and Jack, Joan, myself and another friend, Alex Katz, went there. Alex was a Village artist, a real "character" who sketched all the time and painted anything to buy art supplies—a true painting addict. For instance, he painted Minetta's walls in exchange for a discount on food and drink. There he painted a life-sized mural of a bar on the wall behind the bartender, where the customers looked as though they were staring back at themselves from their barstools. Alex always wore a dirty black beret and a messy smock with charcoal pencils sticking out of the pockets. He loved his wine and he seemed to always be everywhere we were. I favored Minetta's dinners because they put a lot of meat in their spaghetti sauce. I liked their special house salad dressing, too, and for three dollars you even got biscuit tortoni for dessert. People drifted in, sat with us, talked, and then moved on— mostly artists. Jack would sometimes play chess in the corner. Jack loved chess. He was good at all brain games, but he did not like cards or anything to do with gambling.

Although Jack wanted to go into the Navy Air Corps, he decided to join the merchant marine with Henri, because the money was there, and it would enable him to be based in New York. That way we could live together and he could write.

chapter 7

That party was our last night together as a group. The following day we all went back to our own separate parts of the
United States—most of us traveling by train. I took the
"Empire State" train leaving from Grand Central Station and
had to stand a good part of the way. As the war ground on they
did not have reserved seats because the soldiers had priority. I
got into Detroit late that same night and took a cab the nine
miles to Grosse Pointe. At the time I lived in the downstairs
of a two-family flat in Grosse Pointe Park with my mother and
younger sister, Charlotte, who was in high school and had her
own circle of friends. The majority of people in Grosse Pointe
didn't lack anything, except enough things to spend their
money on.

My Grosse Pointe friends were a very close-knit group, so
exclusive that we even made up our own language, "turkey

Edie Parker on the far right with some of her friends in Grosse Pointe, Michigan.

talk," as we called it. It was spoken by only a few and never understood by outsiders. It came in handy at school because the schoolteachers never caught on. In my schoolgirl days I had never read any books for pleasure and rarely even cracked a schoolbook. Now I was thrilled by the new world of literature Jack was opening up for me.

That Christmas found me working downtown in Detroit's biggest department store, J.L. Hudson's, along with three of my closest girl friends. I was hired to sell ties for $1.00 each on a 12% commission, plus $20.00 a week straight pay for a six-day schedule. Lee Donnelly was pushing handkerchiefs and my other friend, Jane Beebe, was in gloves. We all worked down in the basement. Another friend, Mildred Fisher, had a job in the office on the top floor. We would often argue over who would drive my mother's 1935 gray, four-door Ford to work. What a wonderful car—straight on the floor stick. I shifted with my leg wrapped around the stick. It's funny that Jack never could learn to drive. He was always amazed that everyone in Grosse Pointe did it so easily, almost like breathing.

Lee and Beebe knew of my plans to move back to New York and get my own apartment. Beebe was all for it, but Lee didn't think too much of the idea. I had a lot of good times in Detroit with my friends. When working downtown it was our habit to go to the Statler Hotel's Terrace Room for a drink Saturday afternoons. I loved a good Tom Collins and would have a ball, sometimes ending up in a hotel room upstairs. Not for sex, but believe it or not, for a shower. Around five of us would rent a room, then we would turn the showers on full blast and plug up the drains. As the water rose we would soap up both ourselves and the bathroom floor. With soap everywhere, we'd get down on our butts and slide all over the tiled shower room laughing hysterically. Invariably, everything would flood and the manager would come banging on the door, putting an end to it all. I learned that trick at the Detroit Yacht Club when I lived on my father's boat before I was twelve. It wasn't half the fun the Statler was, though. Jack always talked about doing this with Beebe and me. After getting spanking clean, we would head home. Being on your feet eight hours a day at Christmas in Hudson's was no picnic, and I was glad when the job came to an end after the holidays. I managed to make some decent money though; I think everyone in Detroit bought one of those damn ties.

When it was time to go, my friend Lee volunteered to drive me to the train station. I wore a huge yellow straw hat with a veil. I remember my clothes were on hangers that kept getting caught on everything, and I carried my radio under one arm and my suitcase in the other, all the while teetering on high heels. My mother kept saying, "No, you can't go," but I was young and I was gone. Lee was distressed by it all, but I told her that if she wouldn't drive me, I would take a cab. Oh my, what I would give today to have that confidence back and live my life over. I would never have left Jack.

It was a cold, gray day in January when the train pulled out of the station. Believe me, it was no tearful goodbye. I remember that the train was always too slow going; too fast coming back. I made that trip frequently over the next six years, to replenish both my body and my wardrobe. Grosse Pointe was where the dentist, doctor, food and clean bathrooms were, but New York City was where my heart was.

I decided I wanted to look for a different kind of job when I returned to the city. Jack's one desire was to write, but he also knew he'd have to enter the service. We were all very patriotic. I knew Jack was being influenced by his friend G.J., who was in the Coast Guard, but Henri Cru was a great influence, too, and he was all for Jack joining the merchant marine. For my part, I felt a better job would help pay for the new apartment we were trying to find with Joan.

It was a sad time for Jack and me. We never knew how long it would be before we would see each other again. He wasn't going to school anymore, and it would be hard for him to get back to New York.

When the train finally arrived at Grand Central Station I

got a cab directly to Gram's apartment. I could hardly contain myself. Jack would be arriving the next day from Lowell and we had a date to meet at the Lion's Den, the Columbia dining room. There was a message waiting from Joan asking me to call her in Albany. I used the phone in the back of the lobby behind the elevator even before I went up to Gram's. Joan said she had found an apartment right around the corner and had put a deposit down in her name and Mr. and Mrs. Jack Kerouac. I couldn't believe it. Everything was going to work out after all. Our plans were all falling into place. I asked if she had written to Jack? She had not. So I thought, what a surprise I would have for him. Joan said it was partially furnished and we talked about the fun we'd have fixing it up. I hung up, exhausted from the trip and went upstairs to bed.

The next morning while taking Rex for his walk, I went over to our new place at 420 W. 119th Street, between Amsterdam and Morningside Drive, and looked it over. It was quite a swanky building. It even had a little yard in front with a half-round walk and a lot of windows into the lobby. There was a switchboard with a pleasant operator who handed me a key. I went up in a gold elevator and the man let me out on the fourth floor. What class, I thought. I opened the door and walked inside. There was one bedroom, a big living room and a good size kitchen. Four huge windows overlooked a very bright and cheery courtyard. The fire escape spanned the width of the apartment—like a porch. You could step out any window and take in the sun if you felt like it.

Later I learned that all of the apartments that looked onto the courtyard were occupied by Julliard students. Most times you could hear sopranos practicing, pianos and violins playing, even canaries singing. It was like being on a Broadway stage with the cast, all for $44 a month. I was excited; it was my first apartment on my own and I'd be sharing it with my love, Jack, as well. My whole being sang with the soprano in the courtyard.

Late that afternoon I met Jack at the Lion's Den. As usual he had a Lucky Strike cigarette dangling from his lips and was leaning in the doorway, very suave, wearing a heavy red-and-black plaid wool shirt with dark pants. He hugged me with one arm and smelled so good. Picking up his duffel bag, we walked across Broadway into the West End where he sat me down and got us two beers. We held hands across the table as I told him about the apartment. Could there ever be a more wonderful day?

Then Jack told me he was leaving for the navy—soon. He had decided to sign up after being at sea on the *S.S. Dorchester* to Greenland with the merchant marines. Suddenly the war was about to affect us directly. I realized that the trade-off for my dream come true was that it would be temporary. We had to be alone, our love was choking us, we wanted each other desperately.

The next day we went to our new apartment and I almost felt like a new bride. We were Mr. and Mrs. here and they addressed us as such. I can't recall if there was a bed, but I do remember a mattress and a candle. Comfort was not on our minds, however. Later we did get a trundle bed that was all iron and popped up to make a poor man's king size. It was horrible, but we were in heaven.

chapter 8
. . .

Our first night living together was New Year's Eve, the last day
of 1942, and everything and everybody was consumed by the
war. All our friends would be at the West End that night
because we all knew it might be the last time we were together.
Jack and I wanted to have everyone up to the apartment for
New Year's breakfast, so we went shopping. Jack went to the
liquor store for booze and wine while I went to the food store
for bacon, eggs, butter, bread, peanut butter, coffee and milk.
We had the best time shopping and afterwards we stopped at
the deli where they made some corned beef on rye sandwiches
for us. After buying mustard, pickles, ripe olives and smoked
oysters, we strolled back to the apartment with our arms full.

Beethoven's Festival played on WEXL all afternoon while
we napped. We had one radio in the bedroom and another in
the large living/bedroom. We nibbled on a sandwich, drank

Jack Kerouac, Columbia University, 1943.

beer, popped olives and talked as the sun left the courtyard. We discussed New Year's and what we would do afterwards. Jack shaved while I went back to Gram's to get my clothes. It was all so impermanent domestic. I had on my red velvet dress with long pearls, black suede high heels and faux diamond earrings. They were set in a cluster that went up the outer rim of my ear in a half moon that caught the light and Jack loved them. He had a wonderful habit of putting his arm around me at shoulder height in back of my neck and lovingly fingering my ear lobe. It always sent sparks through me.

It was Jack's custom to just sit and think. He was never in a hurry for anything. He loved to be with me—alone—have a few sips of wine and nibble. I put trays on the floor or on a hassock, and it was much like camping out on a plush carpet with lots of cushions. Our conversations were about our youth; the things he wanted to be (a writer), what I wanted to be (with him), our friends, their love lives and our dreams. We had a lot of things to talk about. At one point we had even started to analyze each other because I was taking a course in psychology.

When we finally got to the West End that night for the party, everything was really beautiful. There were Christmas lights in the front windows and it was romantically dark inside, lit only by candles in the booths.

Fitz was at the bar, more in the bag already than Uncle Dunc and drooling over some blonde. Dunc came to our booth with Dicki Goebel, and I slid in next to Dunc while Jack went up to get us all drinks. Dunc asked me about my Michigan Christmas, then told me Fitz and he had enlisted in the army and were waiting to be called up. We were all still somehow optimistic about the future. Jack sat down with the drinks and started to talk about what was happening. Jack told them he was trying to get into the navy, preferably the Air Corps. Fitz gave me a hug, held my hand and started to tell me how much he missed me. Fitz acted as if he was interested, but it didn't phase Jack in the least—this was Fitz. Then two men I knew from Asbury Park, both named Bill, came in the door. One had dark curly hair and the other had straight blond hair. They were muscular, well developed young men who had spent most of their lives fishing in the surf. Now it was time for them to go out and sail the oceans of the world. Henri Cru had told them about the merchant marine and they had come to ask Jack about the ins and outs of the union hall. We were happy to see them.

All of a sudden, Joan arrived and Uncle Dunc's face lit up. Now everyone was there, so we drank up before going downtown to welcome in the New Year. Times Square was teeming with everyone in the world all crammed into one place. Before we knew it, it was midnight and everyone went mad, hugging and kissing. Thousands and thousands all shouting "Happy New Year!" as they pushed and shoved themselves around Times Square. We had made about three laps by 2:00 A.M. when we left for the subway home.

Once again the train seemed to be filled with students singing. As we walked up the stairs onto Broadway, Jack put his arm around my shoulders and spoke earnestly to the two Bills. I thought of Henri off at sea, alone. He had been writing to my grandmother and had, by that time, turned his attention to my sister.

Joan, Dunc and Fitz were walking ahead of us and it started

to snow. The college campus turned into a fairyland as we walked along the red brick sidewalks. Spotlights shown on the grand, marble-pillared buildings, it was all so lovely. Best of all, we were going home to our own brand new apartment; we were real New Yorkers now. The feeling of belonging to New York has never left me, and I know it never left Jack either. The doorman was gone for the night and no one was on elevator duty so we had to climb the stairs. Jack raced ahead with the key to turn on the lights. He was beaming with pride for his new home as we all walked in. Joan and I started everything going in the kitchen. I did the bacon and toast. Jack was doing his part by making coffee as he had learned on the *Dorchester*. My, it was super—good and strong. Joan was in charge of the eggs and potatoes. I never knew anyone who could cook eggs like Joan. We always tried when she wasn't there, but it was no use. She said her secret was to "cook them slow." Before long it was time to eat, so we all grabbed trays, silverware, plates and toilet paper for napkins and had a feast.

Joan and I put the dishes in the sink to soak. Then out came the wine and fancy glasses. Jack loved good glasses. Eventually we were all stretched out on the floor starting to fall asleep— warm, full, tired and happy. The music of "Horace Haight and his Musical Knights" was on the radio in the distance, playing all the oldies.

chapter 9

It was time for Jack, Joan and me to get down to the business
of finding jobs to support our new apartment. We started to
think about what might be the easiest way to make money.
During the war, many jobs which normally would have been
reserved for men were available to women, and they paid good
money. Jack wanted to get a job that was nearby and would
take up the least amount of his time. Joan and I agreed that his
time was to be spent on writing, that was most important. For
a while Jack found part-time work at Columbia's dining hall
as a waiter. That way he figured he could also smuggle food
home for us. Joan and I focused on the want ads. Joan got a
job addressing envelopes and typing. Jack helped her with it
when he was able to. Joan also made extra cash correcting students' papers for spelling and punctuation—she was a brilliant
woman.

I have always been much more physical and mechanical, maybe it came from having grown up in Detroit surrounded by all the automotive people. One thing I could do was drive. I thought I could drive anything, so I got a job working as a longshoreman. Jack had seen a notice for workers on the board in the merchant marine union hall. All of the longshoremen were being drafted and shipping out, leaving no one with an operator's license to take over the important job of loading the ships. I started working a 10-hour shift at the New York Port of Embarkation on the Brooklyn army base. I made eighty-five cents an hour, which was not bad back then. I drove a forklift, tow motors, and Clarks [hi-lo] large and small. When you drive these it's usually with a wooden palette loaded with cargo and almost always backward. As a result, today I can drive backward better than I can forward. Back then I drove an electric, four-wheel hi-lo that carried six cargo pallets at a time down the pier, backing up to the winch which picked up each palette and hoisted them onto the ship. I loved the job but it was a twelve-hour day, including the commute each way—I was exhausted. I popped vitamins and began to eat like a longshoreman as well. It was wintertime so I would wear eight sweaters plus navy wool sailor's pants and a pea jacket. Women didn't wear slacks back then—that was only in the movies, you couldn't even buy them. When I was at work I looked like an overstuffed wrestler, but it was cold on the docks down by the ocean and I only cared about staying warm.

Jack and I became friends with my boss, Roderick C. Bacote, a very kind, sharp black man. He often came to the apartment for drinks and spoke to Jack about shipping out. Secretly, I hoped it would be a while before Jack would have to leave me. Roderick always tried to give me the easier jobs, one of which was working in the warehouse loading elevator. The hardest things to handle were coffee and sugar because they were in bags and were easily spilled, but I loved it because it was a challenge.

One day, on the 7:00 A.M. shift, that all changed for me. I found an army guard in the warehouse who had shot himself in the head. I had to go home early that day. Jack was also shaken up, and it brought a new, personal aspect of the war into our lives. From then on I tried to avoid working in the warehouse. When I worked at night, we would finish loading the liberty ships and watch the soldiers board. Then we'd watch them set sail down the East River to join a convoy out in the Atlantic. Sometimes, way off in the distance, we could see a glow on the horizon and hoped it wasn't our ship being hit by a torpedo. We knew the German U-boats and wolf packs were patrolling the coast at night.

They were out there all right. From Asbury Park, looking over the blackout fence installed along the shore to block the lights on the coastline, we could see enemy submarines cruising on top of the water. They were going up and down the Jersey shore as bold as brass, silhouetted in the light from the moon. In the houses along the coast, the only lights we could use at night were dim red or green, and it was a law that all shades be drawn.

Our New York apartment was always humming after classes and work. Fitz (mentioned in a lot of Jack's books as "Fitzpatrick") wrote flowery poetry and had a thing for me. Uncle Dunc was very fond of Joan. The two would discuss Freud, Kafka, Marx and politics over kummel and listen to Bach. Fitz and I liked jazz, Beethoven, beer, the West End and "FUN." Jack liked all of it, but not half as intensely as the rest of us. Fitz seemed to have mostly bad luck with his sex life. I remember one night he picked up one of the many West End barflies, a girl about thirty whose name was Mary, and brought her back to our apartment and into bed. Early the next morning he told us that she must have had on six dresses and by the time he got the fourth one off, he fell asleep. We roared with laughter—that was Fitz.

Uncle Dunc and Fitz went into the army at camps near Washington, D.C. but would often come back to Columbia when they were on leave. I remember Dicki was always kind of lost. He would take Joan and me out bar hopping to all the big hotels and swank places—The Ritz, The Savoy, The Astor, The Plaza—hoping that sailors would talk to us. They did, but Dicki never could understand why they didn't latch on to him. Then "Dickibird," as we called him, managed to get a government job in Washington and I hope stopped his "cruising" life and found his heart's desire.

Seymour Wyse was Jack's very best friend after Henri Cru. They had all attended Horace Mann together. Seymour was a big, rumbling, rambling man. The image that comes to mind is of a St. Bernard puppy. He was a genius—at just what, I never did know, but Jack told me he was smart. He was from England and his father, a famous scientist, sent Seymour to school in New York to escape the London blitz. He and Jack were very close and they shared Seymour's one and only interest, jazz. The new Negro jazz ("dirty blues") was loud, fast, strong, slow and sweet. Nothing was ever written down, so the musicians would just go in front of an audience and "blow."

They might play "Sunny Side of the Street" for forty-five minutes, of which I would recognize maybe ten minutes. Seymour, Jack and I loved it.

Jack went down to the union hall whenever he could. His daily routine was to write all night long, then wake me up around dawn. I would make him a gigantic breakfast with milk instead of coffee. Rarely did he discuss what he wrote with me, as a matter of fact, early in the morning was a quiet time for him. Then he would get ready for bed and sometimes I would go back with him depending on my work schedule. He had a high body heat and he slept on his stomach with one arm in the air or above his head. So on a three-quarter bed there wasn't enough room for me to "spreadoutsky," as Jack would say.

Usually he would wake up around noon and go to his job or to the union hall, or sometimes he'd just read at home or in the Columbia library. When he went out, he left me notes with doodles or drawings. None of us liked to call or talk on the telephone. I am still the same way, but in Jack's later years he developed diarrhea of the mouth when it came to long distance calls. His family in Lowell wrote him all the time, his mother almost everyday. Jack would answer once a week. He wasn't big on letter writing in those days.

Well, finally the dreaded day came. As was his fashion, Jack never said a word about it beforehand. When he had something to tell me, he would be especially sweet and talkative. He'd try to get me to not go to work and plan the whole day, sleeping in late after a wonderful night of lovemaking. Sometimes we'd take a bath together. Usually, the bathroom was Jack's private domain and to allow me in there was really something special. Then we would go to a favorite place for lunch, often Jack Delaney's on Sheridan Square. This day, after lunch, we walked around to the art galleries and made our way to the Museum of Modern Art for tea and dessert on the patio. I knew something was up so I asked Jack what was on his mind, but he replied simply, "Nothing."

We rode uptown on the Riverside Drive double-decker bus and headed toward Columbia. We got off at 96th Street and walked, holding hands, over to Broadway where we went into Barton's Chocolates and bought a two-pound box of truffles. Jack adored truffles. As we started to walk up Broadway we stopped in a pet shop, another one of my favorite places. We looked and petted and cooed, when all of a sudden Jack said, "Isn't that little black puppy cute?" "Yes," I said, "It's a cocker spaniel."

Jack took it out of the cage and put it in my arms. It was just four months old and weighed about twelve pounds. We asked the price—it was $6.00. "Why so little?" I asked. "No papers, last of the litter and a female," the shop owner told us.

Without hesitation, Jack said, "We'll take it," and handed the man the $6.00. I was dumbfounded because Jack's impulses were rare. We got a rope and started to walk home, now broke. That darling little thing couldn't walk very far, so we took turns carrying her. That is when Jack chose to tell me that he had been posted to a ship. He would be leaving soon for Lowell, then Boston, and then aboard the *S.S. Dorchester* to who knew where. So that was the reason for the puppy, I thought, to keep me busy so I wouldn't be lonesome. What could I do except be grateful for our last day together and the puppy? We named our little black dog, Woof-it. As soon as we got back to our apartment Jack began to pack for his trip.

Since I had made up with my grandmother after the death of my grandfather, my plans were to help her pack to move to Asbury Park for the summer. Woof-it and I would be able to visit her on long weekends. Fortunately Woof-it got along with grandmother's dog, Rex. In fact, Woof-it was the only dog who ever did.

I speculated as to where Jack would be sailing— Russia maybe, or possibly England. We worked out a

Edie and Woof-it, New York, 1943.

code. He would mention several places in his letters and then say goodbye in the language of the country of his ship's destination so I would know where he was going. That way the censor would never catch on (today it sounds so obvious it makes me laugh). When the time came for him to leave, I remember it was warm and the leaves were just appearing on the trees. Woof-it and I walked Jack to the subway entrance, it was a very sad moment for me. We spoke of marriage and hoped for it soon, as we all did in those days. Underneath was an awareness of doom and death. You always felt goodbyes might be just that. To say goodbye was too often permanent during the war.

chapter 10
. . .

Very early that Monday morning I was back on the subway going to my job as a longshoreman. There were cautionary posters in the trains that read, "A slip of the lip could sink a ship," among others. As the weather became warmer I grew more restless. I had worked hard all winter in the cold and felt I needed a rest. Life had become very depressing with Jack and everyone else gone, so I asked my boss for a leave of absence for a few weeks. I wanted to go to Lowell since Jack would be there for another two weeks before he shipped out. I wrote to see if it would be all right with him. Joan volunteered to feed and walk Woof-it, since she was in the apartment more than I was. Jack wrote back encouraging me to come; he had just the place for me to stay, G.J.'s girlfriend Lorraine had her own apartment. I was very excited about seeing Lowell since Jack had told me so many stories, and I was anxious to be with him once more before he left.

The next week Roderick gave me a three-week leave of absence. I decided to take the bus since Jack told me I would see more that way. But, just like a man, he didn't mention how long it would take. I was all day on that bus. We stopped at every "burg" all the way to Lowell. Greyhound was conserving gas so the express busses were not running. Lowell was an industrial town on the Merrimack River, full of French Canadians and Greeks who worked for minimum wages in the textile mills.

When I got into Lowell around dinnertime, Jack was waiting, per usual, with a cigarette dangling from his mouth and love in his eyes. He waited for my bag and asked me the usual questions. How was Woof-it, Joan, Fitz, Uncle Dunc and everyone at the West End bar?

I noticed he was more nervous than usual. I supposed it was because he was with a strange girl in his hometown. We checked my bag at the bus depot. Jack said Lorraine had a car and we could go back later to pick it up. She and G.J. were waiting for us at her house in Pawtucketville, a section of Lowell. We took a local bus right from the depot. It was dark by that time and I remember it as a bleak ride, with very few stores along the way, only wooden, apartment-like flats that were very short on lights. I was used to the bright lights of Broadway and even with the blackout in Asbury Park, you could still see fairly well. Here it seemed pitch black. You could barely see the curb or sidewalk, much less the street signs. It was all very spooky, so I snuggled close to Jack. After a twenty-minute ride, he took hold of my hand and we got off the bus. I thought it strange that the people on the bus never spoke to us or to one another. Nor did the bus driver call out the streets as they do in New York City. Everything around me was mysterious; the houses little more than black silhouettes. The smell of spring was in the air, but the wind was still cold. We had to button up—Jack in his navy pea jacket, and I in my camel-hair coat. Jack held my hand and led me at a fast clip over a wooden boardwalk-type bridge. The water rushing beneath made it feel even colder. There weren't any cars driving by, just darkness. Once across we turned up a side street where the houses were tiny. Just a minute later we went up the walk to one of those small, dark houses and Jack pushed the door open without ringing. He knew precisely where he was going—into the kitchen. Inside was G.J. in his coast guard uniform, dark, tall, full of smiles and welcoming gestures. He was very good looking and had an aura about him like Jack, a mysterious attraction that you could not define. He put a glass of beer in my hand and introduced me to Lorraine, a beautiful woman with a dark complexion and curly black hair. She wore an apron as she peeled potatoes over the newspaper-lined sink and said hello. Lorraine apologized for not shaking my hand; she seemed very friendly and nice. Then her small son came into the kitchen and held out his hand to me very shyly and said something I don't recall. He was all eyes and about six years old. I wondered, of course, but did not ask who the father was. We sat around the kitchen table for a while and drank our beer. Loraine kept laughing as she peeled and we all got along just fine. Jack seemed so proud of me, I thought he would burst.

It was the end of the week, so Jack and G.J. made plans for the weekend. We would stay in that night and then they'd drive me around Lowell tomorrow. Jack had someone special he wanted me to meet. Saturday night we would go to a "roadhouse" where they all went, out on the highway near a lake. Since Jack did not mention his parents, neither did I, although I had hoped to see them. I was happy enough just to be with him in his home town. We had a wonderful meal with prune whip for dessert. Besides being beautiful, I discovered that Lorraine was also a good cook. Afterward, all four of us got up to do the dishes. I washed while Jack and G.J. dried. Then I reminded Jack about my suitcase, it was a heavy leather thing that weighed a ton. G.J. and Jack offered to drive to the bus station to collect it, so off the two of them went. For once, I was content to just sit and talk to Lorraine.

We put her little boy to bed after giving him a splashing bath. Lorraine and I went back downstairs where she showed me my room. There was a double bed so I wondered if Jack would be sleeping with me. After a couple of hours the boys came back, a little loaded, dragging that monster suitcase. Jack carried it upstairs and I heard him bang it on the floor in the large bedroom right above our heads. George (G.J.) sat next to Lorraine on the couch and when Jack came down, he sat in the rocker and gazed at me. It was great to feel how exciting little things can be. Then G.J. took Lorraine's hand and they retired to the bedroom next to the kitchen. Suddenly both Jack and I seemed shy. He asked me if I wanted to take a walk or go to bed. Since neither of us could speak what was on our minds, I went over and took his hand. He sprang from the rocker and kissed me with such a torrent of passion that I could hardly catch my breath. Then we went to bed in each other's arms and it was a long time before he rolled over on his stomach and fell asleep.

chapter 11
. . .

The next morning Jack came in to wake me. He was already fully dressed in his lumberjack style, sitting on the bed, taking me in his arms to kiss me awake. "What time is it?" I asked. "After ten," Jack said. Then I heard, and smelled, breakfast being prepared. I went into the warm bathroom where Jack had put an electric heater on for me, and dressed. There was a knock at the door and there stood Jack with coffee for me and a beer for himself.

We ate a huge breakfast together. This time Lorraine and I did the dishes alone while Jack and G.J. drank beer and argued about where we would drive to see the sights. G.J. was perturbed that Jack had someone for me to meet who he didn't know.

In Lowell, Jack had two separate groups of friends. There were his drinking, going to sport events and chasing girls, bud-

dies and G.J. was of that group. Then there were the intellectual, sensitive types who Jack also enjoyed being with. They
had mad poetry readings and heated conversations about
books and writers. G.J. and his group resented that group and
called them "sissies."

Jack's personality fit into many categories—that was the
kind of man he was. The navy discharged him, in fact, for
being schizoid, for having a split personality. In other words,
one side was all man, while the other side was all intellectual—
a poet and a dreamer. Sometimes one side of Jack would take
over the other side and he would become depressed and
melancholy; his family called him moody. I always ignored all
his moods, and he was far too interested in everything to stay
long in any depression.

I went upstairs to freshen up, grateful to have my turn in the
bathroom before Jack took it over for one of his long sieges.
Sometimes he would stay in there for two hours or longer,
absorbed in the Bible or Shakespeare. While living with him,
I often had to sneak into the "Kerouac Room" whenever the
opportunity presented itself.

But now he was impatient and knocked on the door. "Let's
go," he said and so off we went. Jack and I sat in the back seat
and were chauffeured by G.J. who sat up front alone. We
started for Lupine Road in Centralville. This, Jack explained,
was the street where he was born. The houses were white clap-
boards, all less than three stories with porches. Some had
garages and large old trees, and the streets had no curbs. Then
we drove to an area of five-story tenements, all tired, white-
painted, wooden structures. They sat on a large hill
overlooking a park and a huge hole, which turned out to be the

city's dump. Being from flat Detroit, the hill seemed like a mountain to me. We drove down the winding hill two short blocks to Sarah Avenue where Jack said he had lived when he was in elementary school. A short drive later and we were back at Lorraine's drinking a quart bottle of beer from Dixie cups. By then it was early afternoon and we were all ready for lunch. Lorraine had heated Campbell's tomato soup in a large pan and made lobster salad to put on hot dog buns. Boy oh boy, was it delicious! That is the thing that always recaptures Lowell in my mind: lobster hotdog-bun sandwiches.

After lunch Jack and I went for a walk along the Merrimack. That stretch of the river was slow-moving and wide, with steep banks and a well-worn path beside it. We strolled along the path until we came to a curve in the river, and there we ran into someone sitting on a tree stump. After saying hello, Jack introduced me. "This is my friend, Billy Hardy. He lives in that house on the top of the hill." We all sat down and talked about Billy's recent enlistment in the army. Jack and Billy decided they could write to each other using our New York address and I would forward their letters. They talked of how they might cope with the pending regimentation and what they would read as well. An hour went by quickly before Billy had to leave; his aunt would be looking for him, he said. As we slowly retraced our steps, Jack told me that Billy's uncle was high up in the Catholic Church. He also told me of Billy's uncle's wonderful library and how he and Billy had been borrowing books from it for years.

Two more of Jack's friends were sitting on the porch waiting for him when we got back. Jack introduced me and I said a fast hello before going into the house to help Lorraine peel potatoes for dinner. We talked about where we were going that night and what we should wear. She was going to wear men's fatigues that she had altered to fit her. I had some slacks from Best & Co. on Fifth Avenue which they sold as a novelty, and I decided to wear them. They were navy blue with pockets in front, pleats, a zipper on the side and full pant legs. With that I wore a yellow Brooks pullover sweater with my initials "F.E.P." embroidered on the front.

We all went to the roadhouse that was out in the country surrounded by empty cottages. The joint was huge and packed with people by the time we arrived. There was a large dance floor with tables all around it and a raised stage for the band. The bar was in the back, too. Everyone seemed to know Jack and G.J.

We found a table with about twelve other people who bought pitchers of beer and baskets of pretzels. The men were in uniforms, mostly army. Jack said they were all home on leave. The band started to play loudly and I thought, badly. It was so loud, no one could talk. Jack, G.J. and four others all went to the john together, which I thought seemed odd. I asked Lorraine and she told me that since it was a beer and wine only place, they had a secret whisky bar in the men's room. Right then, I knew it was going to be a lonesome night. While he was gone a fellow came up and asked me to dance, so I did. Unfortunately, I can't dance, so my turn on the floor was brief. By the time the poor guy had finished trying to push me around that dance floor, Jack was back at the table laughing because of my bad dancing. We had a good time, but I had a little too much to drink, so Jack had to help me out of the place. An icy rain was falling when we got to the parking lot.

As G.J. and Lorraine got into the front and started the motor I slipped under the car in the mud and hit my head, just as he put it in reverse. All I know is that Jack pulled me out, right in the nick of time. Jack and I referred to this incident as the time he saved my life, which I've always believed to be true.

chapter 12

. . .

The following day Jack and I took a train into Boston and got off at North Station. I wanted to see the battleship, the *S.S. Constitution*. My ancestor, Donald Mackay, had built it one hundred and fifty years ago. My grandfather had still been in the steel-making end of the naval business when he died and I was thrilled to see "Old Ironsides" at last.

From there Jack and I trudged across Charlestown Bridge and up State Street to the Italian neighborhood, where we hopped onto a cute little streetcar. Jack was proud to be showing me his Boston. It seemed his long R's were rolling more than I'd ever noticed before, so I began to speak with a western twang in response to him. I used a lot of "I reckons" as a way of acknowledging his exaggerated accent. We were always playfully putting each other on in one way or another.

At the end of the mall in Boston is Old North Church

where they hung the lanterns that warned of a British attack, "one if by land and two if by sea." Jack recited the entire Paul Revere poem to me from memory. Next door we visited the Old Corner Bookstore. A plaque commemorated the fact that Emerson, Hawthorne, Thoreau, Whittier, Harriet Beecher Stowe, Julia Ward Howe, all the New England writers, had come there during its history. Jack wanted me to learn about his background, what and where he came from. All of our emotions were clouded by the fact that he was going off to the war, and so we clung to each other. I had a feeling of thirst with no way to quench it, a sense of immediacy. He took my hand and led me out of the bookstore while I dreamed that someday his books would be on those very shelves.

We walked back toward the waterfront to a restaurant that was huge and bleak, Durgin Park. "Dirty Durgin Park," Jack called it. He always played with words. But in spite of his nickname, the food was wonderful. We ate fish chowder with lots of oyster crackers, served in a steaming blue and white soup tureen with soup bowls to match. The crackers came in a huge quart bowl. Next we went on to Boston Common with its lawns full of beautiful flowers and trees. How peaceful it all seemed in a world that was falling apart. We sat on a bench near the pond and looked out to a swinging suspension bridge. The ducks and swans swam around waiting for Jack to toss them the oyster crackers he had filled the pockets of his corduroy jacket with. I watched him, imagining how handsome he would look in his navy uniform, with brass buttons and a decorated hat. Some couples paddled by in boats, but the ducks paid no attention to them. Jack said, "Let's go. There's more I want to show you."

We went into King's Chapel burial ground where Jack pointed out the grave of William Dawes, the real savior of the Colonial troops. His tombstone was surrounded by a lot of British soldier's graves. As we walked back through the Common, Jack told me it was fifty acres and had once belonged to William Blackstone, who used it as a pasture to graze his cows. In the distance you could see some lovely old brick houses with ornate, shiny black iron fences and gorgeous brass knockers and lanterns. Jack told me it was Beacon Hill, where families like the Cabots and Lodges lived.

We even went to S.S. Pierce, a beautiful grocery store in Boston. The clerks all wore white butcher aprons with their dark suits. I bought some canned corn and tomatoes to take back to Joan, plus a wedge of New England cheddar cheese cut from a huge fifty-pound wheel which they kept wrapped in heavy wax paper.

Jack and I headed through the Back Bay section to Copley Square to meet G.J. before I caught my train back to New York. The Copley Plaza Hotel had lovely old furniture and every chair had a small velvet cushion. We sat at the bar and had a drink while we waited for G.J. Jack had to go to Scully Square to see about his naval assignment after I left. We both felt terrible because it would be our first real separation. When G.J. finally arrived, I said goodbye and left for the station.

The train ride back was a melancholy one for me. I always carry a large purse in case I am gone all day. In it is usually a book to read and a change of shoes—plus an apple, a sandwich (usually cheese) and a few pieces of hard candy. People always laughed at Jack for carrying his toothbrush around in his shirt pocket, but I knew how he felt. When he reached for a cigarette it always fell out. You knew he had someplace permanent to stay when his toothbrush was not in his pocket.

In an hour we were in Worcester and the conductor called out in his New England accent, "Wooster." To me it was a boring-looking town. Jack said his father had gone there often as a traveling salesman. After a twenty-minute stop, the train continued to Springfield, Hartford and New Haven.

After switching tracks in New Rochelle to go through Harlem, we stopped at 125th Street where I got off at last and grabbed a cab to the apartment. Joan said my grandmother had dropped over, checking on me. Gram was very suspicious and I didn't like that. Joan had told her I was working. I walked past her apartment, but since her lights were off, I didn't go up and decided I'd go back in the morning.

Jack and I had been sleeping on a mattress and box springs laid on the floor of the living room since Joan used the bedroom. Joan and I began to talk about getting a larger apartment, since Jack was going to be there permanently. Almost at once we began looking for notices on the bulletin board at the Columbia bookstore. Summer was coming and we'd stand a better chance of finding an apartment, since most students left campus then.

chapter 13

. . .

We tried hard to find a larger place. For nearly two years we had lived on East 119th Street and the time to renew the lease was getting close. We looked for an apartment with at least two bedrooms because Jack and I wanted more privacy.

Out of the blue one Sunday morning, Joan got a telegram from Paul, her husband, saying that he was coming home on furlough. He had been a law student at Columbia when she met him, but now was a soldier stationed in Tennessee. He was getting leave because he had a fungus on his foot from walking in the swamps. Since I had never met him I was a little nervous, and I arranged to stay at my grandmother's so Joan and Paul could be alone.

In the meantime Jack had been sent to boot camp in Norfolk, Virginia. I had gotten a postcard from him telling me how much he hated it. He hoped to qualify as a gunner, since they did not put him in Air Force School. All his friends from Lowell who went in with him at the same time had been assigned to different camps, so he was alone.

I was still working as a longshoreman at the New York Port of Embarkation. My grandmother wrote to my mother in Grosse Pointe telling her that I went to work every day looking like a plumber. I wore Henri's pea coat and his navy bell-bottoms with all those buttons.

It was Henri who kept in touch with my grandmother. He was somewhere off the coast of Africa with Bill Sweeton, one of the two Bill's from Asbury Park. Henri was still mad at me and would not mention my name in his letters to Gram. One time Henri's mother was having tea in Gram's apartment and she snubbed me because I had jilted her darling son. I remember her clearly. She was a tiny, thin woman with brown-gray hair, cut short and curly. She wore a hair net as did all the older ladies back then. I did not find her at all attractive. Mrs. Cru always wore a hat, usually a pillbox type, and dresses from Paris. They were silk and usually one solid, somber color, black or blue. My grandmother wore much gayer light wool dresses and silk prints in browns and wines. I remember they both wore low-heeled shoes, sometimes pumps, but most of the time oxford's. And neither of these ladies cooked; it seemed more economical in New York City to eat out. The grocery stores were not around the corner, but blocks away, and since they both lived in the same building, they usually ate in the tearoom downstairs. The tearoom had about a dozen tables and each bentwood chair had a doily draped over the back. The doilies clung to your coat when you got up, so I was forever returning them. Jack liked the food in the tearoom and the fact that I could charge it to Gram's account. They even served sherbet between the courses, like most of the better places did.

The first time that I returned to our apartment to walk Woof-it, Paul Adams was there. Joan was pleased to introduce us and we sat over coffee and chatted. I found Paul to be very handsome. He had light brown hair and eyes that matched. When he got up from the kitchen table, I saw that he was well over six feet tall with broad shoulders. He spoke very softly with no discernable accent. Come to think of it, neither did Joan.

Paul liked to read. In fact most of the books around the apartment were his. *Semper Lumen* was written in Latin in each of his books. Joan said it meant "the light." Since Paul was lounging and relaxing with Joan, I didn't stay very long. His furlough was only for two weeks while his feet were being treated at Fort Dix.

As I walked back down Amsterdam Avenue, I noticed that the trees had all turned green. It was warm; the daffodils were open and the scent floated up to me from the garden on the corner. You could look right down into the garden from my grandmother's apartment and see all the flowers and trees in blossom. Even in the winter you could see the greenhouse with its abundance of blooms. The exhilaration of being young and walking fast on a New York City street, being without doubts and in love, cannot be described, only felt. And the whipped cream on it all was spring.

chapter 14

. . .

Still searching for an apartment, Joan decided to visit Ruth
and Edmund Clark, friends of ours who lived on Riverside
Drive. Ruth was pregnant and Ed was about to go into the
service, so Joan thought they might be moving. Ruth had
decided to stay and keep her apartment, but she told Joan
about someone who might be moving. After coffee we called
and were told that he was going to leave in a few months, and
he gave us the address, 421 W. 118th Street, Apartment #62, so
that we could go right over to see it. We rang the bell, were
let in, and found the stairs at the back of the building. There
were two apartments to every floor and the apartment we had
come to see was on the top floor in the rear. It was a steep
climb for us, so we stopped to rest. Wow! What a climb! We
knocked on the door and it swung open by itself, so we called
hello and went in. A long, narrow corridor stretched out

before us. The kitchen was first, then a small bedroom where a child was playing with a cat. Next was a huge bath, all white tile with a free-standing tub with feet. Joan's eyes lit up. Then another bedroom, bigger than the first, and at the end of the long hall, yet another bedroom. We continued through a set of sliding doors into a large double-size living room that was filled with sunlight pouring in through huge windows. A woman was sitting on a chair basking in the sun. She was pregnant like Joan, and we all sat on a small platform in the open window. The woman told us they would be leaving pretty soon, and without hesitating we thanked her and went down to see the super. We immediately signed the lease as Mrs. Paul Adams and Mrs. John Kerouac for $42 per month plus utilities. Joan gave him the first month's rent and I gave him the last.

Apartment building at 421 West 118th Street, New York.

It would still be a few months before we could move in and Joan's baby was due in the meantime. At the local deli we shared coffee and talked things over. The deli owner said he would save us some cartons for packing, and Joan and I carried some of them back to the old apartment.

Without delay, Joan dove right into packing Paul's books

first. He had a lot of textbooks about law and money. Then she put hers in boxes: all her Steig, Joyce, Proust, Goethe and even Karl Marx. I didn't have much to pack and Jack borrowed most of the books he read from the Columbia library. All I had was a large record collection, so I packed that. Henri Cru had once given me his aluminum Victrola, and Jack had left behind his favorite records, so all those went into boxes, too.

We were so excited about our new apartment that we chatted away while packing. We talked about how we would paint it and what furniture we would put where. There would be a room for Joan's baby, and Jack and I would have privacy too, for a change. That left an extra bedroom we could rent out plus part of the living room, which could be made into another bedroom if we needed it. We had a lot to plan and do.

I was working the night shift at my defense tractor job. Roderick had pulled a lot of strings so I could still work and attend daytime classes. The biggest drawback was that I had to work on Staten Island, which meant taking the subway and ferry both ways.

When the time came, the two Bills helped us move all our stuff to our new home. Henri Cru was out of my life completely, even though my grandmother always kept me informed of his whereabouts, whether I wanted to know or not. Jack was on a voyage to who knew where. He never knew ahead of time, but we used to imagine wild, glamorous ports of call. I think this trip he took was to England, maybe Liverpool.

Once we had settled into the new apartment I was able to socialize more with new friends I had made around campus. I had met a young man by the name of Lucien Carr in one of my art classes. His easel was placed to the right and a little in back of me, but he caught my eye as much as the model. He was taller than Jack and had a thick head of curly, dirty blond hair. I couldn't keep my eyes off of him and I noticed that other girls were also looking at him. He really should have been on the model's stand just as he was, very sloppily dressed with a white cotton shirt, opened at the neck. It had never seen starch and his sleeves were rolled so tightly that you knew he had taken the scissors to them. He wore khaki pants with the legs rolled up and loafers with no socks. Carr seemed to be very intent on his work and noticed nothing else. Then, all of a sudden, he let out a loud whistle and said, "Not bad. Not bad!" admiring his own sketch. Later he walked around the room and looked at everyone's work, completely at ease, not noticing the attention he was attracting. I was spellbound by him; he moved like a cat. His movements were like mercury over rocks. His eyes were slanted, almost oriental, and pure green, so green they dazzled you. Above all, he was unaware of the effect he had on the girls, which made him all the more attractive. As he continued to look at every drawing and each person, he'd say things like "Great" or something nice. You had the feeling that he was interested in you, not himself. When he got to my easel, he stood for a long time in complete silence so I glanced up and noticed that he was looking at me and not my work. Just then the professor called a break and Lucien offered me a cigarette, and from then on we were fast friends.

I made friends with Lucien's girlfriend, Celine Young. She was a lot like me. We had the same background and we dressed in the same way: skirts, saddles, sweaters, and pink oxford cloth men's shirts from Brooks Brothers. She was taller than me, maybe 5'5", and had nice boobs, solidly built. Celine had a shining glow to her complexion and wore very little makeup, just lipstick and Helena Rubenstein Bluegrass cologne. Her greatest asset was her gorgeous, slightly curly, natural blond hair, which I envied. From the beginning I thought she was a terrific gal. Celine, like anyone who is attractive and has the world by the tail, loved to flirt. She had big blue eyes and was full of energy and fun, that's why Lucien adored her so much. They both really fit their looks—their spirit, their bubbling gaiety.

Another of Lucien's classmates named Allen Ginsberg also began hanging out with our crowd around the West End bar, and before very long Allen had met Jack. Allen is difficult to describe. He was younger than all of us—he was seventeen to our twenty years, which is a big gap at that time of your life. He was very naive in many ways and also looked undernourished or underdeveloped. He had small, wiry legs and arms, too long for his body. Allen was always moving, and his large Charlie Chaplin ears stuck out from his head. He reminded me of an Arab with his oily hair and watery eyes, and he had a habit of pushing his dark-framed, horn-rimmed glasses back onto his nose. Allen was a sympathizer and everyone went to him with their troubles, even though he wanted you to feel sorry for his lot in life. Jack would sometimes say, "Look out, Allen will pounce on you like a spider with many legs and then you'll be done for." That seldom happened though, for he realized his neediness was not a charming quality. In spite of that, Allen could be and was sweet, and he was always there for you.

Usually Allen told you what you wanted to hear. He seemed to have an intelligent tongue and an uncanny sixth sense of how to win his personal war with life. You couldn't help but love him because you really felt he loved you, too.

Allen Ginsberg, Columbia University, *ca.* 1943.

Sometimes after you left him, you had doubts, though. He could have been a great politician. Anyway, he chose to be friends with Kerouac, Burroughs and Lucien instead of women. Many of the girls were attracted to Allen for his little boy qualities.

Everyone developed a lasting friendship with another of Lucien's friends named William S. Burroughs. He was also from St. Louis and talked with a slow drawl. Burroughs was a combination of Sherlock Holmes, Wyatt Earp and Abraham Lincoln. He dressed like Holmes, he was fascinated with guns like Earp and he was kind and soft-spoken like Lincoln. He was also sexless like all three. William was like the cavalry, he always came to the rescue, but there was never anyone there to come to his rescue.

One night, Celine Young, John Kingsland, Lucien Carr and I decided to go to see the English Royal Ballet do Swan Lake. John Kingsland was a Columbia student from Brooklyn Heights who lived in a room in the dorms, next door to Lucien. John was a very good looking, suave New Yorker from a wealthy family, and Carr, also from a wealthy background came from St. Louis. Kingsland knew his way around town and in fact, it was he who had gotten the tickets for us. Our seats turned out to be way up in the nearly empty balcony, and as the lights went down, Lucien produced a bottle of wine which he passed around. The original plan was to go out someplace "elegant" to eat afterwards, but we proceeded to get looped and ignored the performance. The stage was a mile away, so I suggested we move closer. As we headed down, I'm afraid we disturbed the few people that were there and then got completely lost in all the corridors. The place was a labyrinth of monstrously long corridors lined with doors that led off to the private boxes. I recall that the carpet was wine-colored with black medallions and looked like a hopscotch pattern, which inspired us to jump wildly from square to square. Lucien stole someone's cape from the cloakroom of the private boxes and impersonated the Phantom of the Opera, taking Celine's eyebrow pencil and drawing a handlebar mustache on himself.

We wandered around the corridors until the music stopped and the halls filled up with foreign-speaking ballet performers, most of whom were Russian. They didn't pay any attention to us at all. They were so scantily dressed that I felt we had joined a bunch of nudists. Since they were all wearing white tights with feathers in their hair and on their tails, they looked like huge White Rock chickens to me. We followed them backstage to a champagne fountain that sat on a long table covered with crystal champagne glasses and a huge bowl of black caviar, lemon wedges and small crackers. Everyone dove in and helped themselves. It was crazy because no one could communicate. We got even more smashed and danced and carried on. When the dancers disappeared to change into their street clothes, we decided it was time to leave.

Our escape route was a huge freight elevator, filled with an assortment of cleaning equipment, and someone—I think myself—said, "Let's take this vacuum cleaner home to Joan . . . she would love it as a gift." It was one of those big upright models, but Lucien was game and dragged it with us through the dark, wet streets. When we boarded a crowded uptown bus, no one even looked surprised to see us, drunk and laughing with our vacuum and the Phantom of the Opera.

Hal Chase, John Kingsland, and Jack Kerouac in
Morningside Park, New York City.

chapter 15

. . .

After a brief stay with me at home, the time came when Jack
was posted to another ship. Joan had gone back to her family's
home in Albany to have her baby. It was Saturday and Jack did
not have to stand watch until the following Monday on the
4 P.M. to midnight shift, so Lucien, Celine, Jack and I discussed what we would do until then. We decided to see the
movie *Lost Weekend*, which was based on a book we had all
read together. It was the first time, to my knowledge, that alcoholism was treated as a sickness and not blight.

"Jackson's book was excellent," Jack said, as he debated the
finer points with Lucien, Allen Ginsberg and John Kingsland.
By that time my father was well on his way into the bottle and
so I had a lot to add to the discussion. They always listened to
me, which was their way with anyone who had something to
contribute.

Then Lucien suggested, "Let's go down to the Village and see Bill Burroughs, maybe go for Chinese?" So off we all went to the subway. Jack said, "I hope we don't run into David Kammerer," and we all agreed. Years earlier, Kammerer had been Lucien Carr's Boy Scout troop leader in St. Louis. The older man had fallen in love with good-looking Lucien and had followed him around the country from one school to another. I always felt that David was creepy and might as well have had cloven hooves and horns growing out of thick, curly red hair. He was the dark cloud that hovered over our lives. David was tall, nearly 6', with muscular long legs. He looked disheveled, like he never had time to zip his fly. Wherever he went, he almost ran, walking with his coat and hair flying. When he climbed the stairs to our apartment, he took them two at a time. Wringing his hands in full-speed anxiety, he was breathless when he spoke. All his waking energy was directed at Lucien, half his age. He drove us all to silence because all he ever wanted to talk about was Lucien. As a result it was best not to say anything at all around him. Needless to say, he was uncomfortable to be around so we avoided him, in fact, Burroughs was the only person who could tolerate him.

We got off the train at Sheridan Square and went straight over to Bill's apartment, but no one was there, so we went to see *Lost Weekend* at the early show. Celine and I went into the lobby while Jack and Lucien got on line for tickets. While Celine had a smoke, she asked me when I was going to go to Asbury Park. I told her Sister would be coming too and invited her to come and visit us there. Then Lucien and Jack came to collect us and we sat down front, seats Jack liked, so he could look up at the people on the screen. He used to say it was so he could "see every pimple on their face and every cavity in their mouth." I remember that the picture was in black and white, and was just a story of a poor, sober drunk, who only wanted another drink. When the movie was over, everyone sat quietly while the lights came on, then ever so slowly we got up and left. Ray Milland had done a fabulous job. Myrna Loy, his girl in the movie was also superb in her part.

We walked to Sheridan Square after the show and commented on how everyone was rushing into all the bars. We weren't eager to get into the heavy drinking, so to speak, so we had a pitcher of beer at Minetta's. Alex Katz came in; since it was the weekend it was a big night for his business. He had his little stool and easel and made pencil sketches of people. If they were enthusiastic about what he did, he would try to make an appointment to do an oil painting of his subject. He was very good at it. He sketched us all; my sister still has the one of herself.

A little later, William Burroughs and David Kammerer found us. They were older, both in their early thirties to our late teens, but age means nothing to your brain, only your ego. As per usual, Kammerer kept leering at Carr. This was my first conscious encounter with a man in love with another man. If it hadn't turned out so tragically it would have been comical. For his part, Lucien was very much in love with Celine. They were always touching, entwined or wrestling with each other. Burroughs disgustedly called them "Flaming Youth." Bill was certainly not one to show his affections in front of others, and neither was Jack, for that matter.

When Jack went to the john, or head as we called it in wartime, Dave grabbed his chair which was between me and

Lucien. Lucien and I both spoke at once, "That's Kerouac's seat!" Then Lucien added, "Beat it." Kammerer just stood up and went back to where he had been, it didn't even phase him. My God, he was a pest! We decided to have Chinese food but wanted to get rid of Dave first, so Lucien said that he had forgotten his wallet back at school. Dave took the bait and offered to go get it for him. I noticed Lucien slip his wallet to Celine under the table, but Dave was on the other side of the table and didn't see it. We told him that we would be at a Chinese restaurant on Bleecker Street when he got back. I should have felt sorry for him. Kammerer had everything going for him—intelligence, money, physique—but he was blind when it came to Lucien. He acted like a groupie around some superstar. It was sickening and hard to take. Burroughs was the only one who held any compassion for him at all, I guess because they had been friends back in St. Louis. Bill never showed his feelings pro or con. As soon as the pitcher of beer was gone, we got up to leave and Lucien hailed a cab. The five of us got in, Bill up front with the driver. Lucien said "Chinatown," which is far from Bleecker Street. Jack started to chuckle about Dave and that was that—no one said "boo."

Bill paid the cab fare, he was nice that way. In the heart of Chinatown we went into a restaurant with a downstairs and upstairs. They had large, paper Chinese lanterns hanging from the ceiling, oak floors and huge, round, wooden tables with captain's chairs to seat ten. We took a table on the first floor of this grand Chinese palace and discovered that the noise above us was deafening. It was the restaurant's custom to encourage the college kids to sing 'til the chandeliers dropped. They were singing with all their lungpower right then. We ordered three pitchers of beer and a group dinner for five with wonton soup and egg rolls to start. Jack loved Chinese food, especially the pork dishes. We all liked hot mustard, so the waiter was always running back for more mustard. Lucien addressed him as, "My good man." We ordered another round of beer and sat back to listen to the singing. For a change they were very good, singing their school songs. The boys from Harvard sang the "Whiffenpoof" song, and we joined in when it was Columbia's turn to sing, "Who Owns New York."

After the meal, the waiter came and asked us for our food

Allen Ginsberg, Lucien Carr, and William Burroughs, 1953.

stamps, then presented us with the check. We all tore out our ration stamps and chipped in some money with Bill paying the most. He carried a cane with a stiletto knife inside it that sprang out with a twist of the ornate, silver dog's head handle. He demonstrated how it worked and stood up and brandished the sword with such enthusiasm that the Chinamen were horrified and ran. "Afraid for their pigtails," Bill remarked, and we fell into stitches of laughter. Jack said *á la* W.C. Fields, "Put your weapons away my good man, or we shall never receive our change." He did, and the poor waiter brought it over meekly. Before long we were gone into the hot August night, heading toward our unforeseen tragic destiny.

We walked to the subway and Burroughs headed back to his apartment in the Village where I hoped Kammerer would join him. When we reached our stop, Lucien and Celine went over to the West End Bar and Jack and I went back to our apartment, climbing the five flights to the sixth floor. Woof-it greeted us there along with our cat, KitKat. I thought about Joan being away to have her baby and I recall feeling a small amount of inadequacy because of my abortion. Jack had never spoken of it after that one blow-up when he first found out. From then on he maintained a grim determination not to speak of it again—his "what's done is done" attitude.

We put Woof-it on her leash and went back down to the street where we walked up Morningside Drive and into the park to let her run. She never went far away, which was good—black dog, black night. It was still hot, so we decided to sit on a bench at the top of Morningside Park, hoping whatever breeze there was would hit us. Then, suddenly, out of the darkness Kammerer came running toward us in an open, dark gray, badly fitting trench coat. He was perspiring, wringing his hands, frantically asking, "Where is Lucien?" Jack lied and told him that we'd left him in the Village and he supposed he was at Bill's. Dave said he must be wrong, he had just come from there. Jack shrugged his shoulders as if to say "I don't know." Then I said something mean, which I have regretted because of what happened next. "He's probably with Celine in her dorm at Barnard. You know Lucien, he gets in anywhere— doors are too conventional." With that Dave streaked off in a panic, as if I had said Lucien was cavorting with the devil. That was the last time I ever saw Dave Kammerer alive.

I learned later that in the early morning hours of August 14, 1944, Kammerer found Lucien in the West End. They were drinking together until the bar closed and then wound up together in Riverside Park. According to reports, Kammerer made threats against Celine and sexual advances toward Lucien. Lucien took out his Boy Scout knife and stabbed Kammerer several times in the heart, then weighted his body and pushed it into the Hudson River. Lucien needed advice and went to Bill's apartment, but Bill advised him to get a good lawyer.

Jack and I were sleeping on a double mattress in the middle of the living room floor the next morning when in popped Lucien. He had the same clothes on as the night before and looked terrible, as if he had had a lover's quarrel with Celine, I thought. Lucien threw himself down on the couch right next to us and mumbled something like, "I just got rid of . . ." He tossed something on the glass-top cocktail table and repeated the statement again, "I just got rid of the old lady." Then he quoted a passage from Shakespeare. I was still half asleep, so Jack nudged me and said, "I think you better make some coffee."

When I came back they were both sitting on the couch speaking in low whispers. There was a pair of horn-rimmed glasses on the cocktail table; I didn't think much about it at the time, I thought they were Lucien's. Since I was up, I went into the bathroom to wash and get ready for the day. When I came out they were still on the couch and Lucien looked like he was going to cry he was so distraught. I asked him if he was all right and began to feel the anxiety in the room. Jack and Lucien finished their coffee and got up to leave. I said, "Do you want breakfast?"

"No, we'll get it out," Jack said and went into the john while Lucien stood outside in the hall looking half-dead. I could feel that something was very wrong, but I thought it was Celine. I approached Lucien and held his hand until Jack came back and started down the stairs. Suddenly Jack turned around and came back to give me a kiss. He said he'd be gone for a while, but that he'd try to get back before his watch began on his ship at four.

That left me to walk Woof-it, and while out I decided to call Joan in Albany and tell her that I thought Lucien had split up with Celine after some terrible fight. I headed for the Columbia bookstore to use the phone but the store hadn't opened yet, so I waited and got my call through to Joan. She couldn't understand my concern, so the conversation turned to more mundane matters like bills to pay, rent due, and so on.

As I walked home I realized that the heat of the day hadn't settled in yet. It felt as if it were going to rain. The sky was overcast, the air was muggy, and if you stuck your tongue out for a time it was kind of salty. Occasionally New York City feels like a seaport, and this was one of those days.

On the way back I stopped at Gram's, knowing she would be getting up and we could go down to the tearoom for breakfast. I gave Woof-it to Ward to watch for a minute and went upstairs. Gram was alone, all dressed up with a hat and gloves when I came in. She was stunning to look at, always dressed elegantly. I sat there feeling a bond between Gram and me, which she must have noticed for she asked, "Are you and Jack planning on getting married?" I was usually very secretive with my family until then; they had a way of throwing things back at me later. But this time I answered, "Yeah, I guess so." She became angry and said, "After what he did, I would think you would get rid of him or marry him, one or the other." Immediately I could tell she was sorry she had said that, but I got up and left. When I got out on the street I wished we hadn't argued.

chapter 16

Back at the apartment, I did my chores. I made the bed and did the dishes and then made coffee, which I put in the refrigerator for later. John Kingsland dropped over, commenting on the hot weather. "Where's Jack?" he asked. I told him he had gone out with Lucien and then we talked about what he had been doing that summer. John stayed with his family in Brooklyn Heights for most of the vacation. As a student at Columbia in the spring he had been spending his spare time with Joan. John was very likeable, and close to Jack, Joan and Lucien. While he and Lucien lived in the dorms, they had met Allen Ginsberg who roomed on the same floor. Although John and Allen were the same age, it was hard to believe, because John was so much more mature in every way.

John wanted to know if Celine was coming in from Pelham, but I said I never knew, she hadn't mentioned it last night. Then we talked about Joan and her problems. He sure missed her, as we all did. Through it all, I kept wondering where Jack could be. It was getting to be lunchtime. John suggested we go to see a movie and cool off in an air-conditioned theater, but I wanted to wait for Jack, since he'd said he'd stop back before going on watch. Then John asked when we planned on getting married, since he knew that we were going to get our blood tests done for our marriage license. I told him Jack wanted to get married in Lowell, even though his parents were now living in Ozone Park, Queens, having moved there to be closer to him just the year before. I really didn't care where the wedding was held, as long as it was kept quiet. I knew my allowance from home would definitely stop if my mother found out I was married. After a while John left and I continued to wait.

Lucien Carr and Celine Young, *ca.* 1944.

Shortly after John went out, Celine came into the apartment. She said she had been at the Columbia fountain waiting for Lucien and asked if I had seen him, so I told her of the strange events earlier that morning. Celine said that she and Lucien had ended up at the West End Bar when they left us the night before. Since she had to get to bed early she had left Lucien there. As she was leaving she noticed that Kammerer was seated at the bar, leering at them. When she walked out he probably went over to Lucien. "Was Lucien loaded?" I asked. "Who can tell when he acts up?" she said. We both wondered what had happened after she left him. Then, still tired, Celine went off to take a nap before dinner.

I stopped at the grocer's and got some fresh supplies for dinner and thought about John Kingsland, who seemed especially lost while Joan was away. I hoped things would get better soon, the war might end or Jack's writing would bear fruit. I dreamed of nothing but marriage and living in Paris on his royalties.

My thoughts turned to the mail, so I hurried home. I was curious because I'd been sending Jack's stories to all of the monthly magazines and *Collier's* hadn't replied yet. Maybe they would buy one of them. But there were no letters and no Jack, either. I took a bath to cool off, then rested and waited.

For dinner I prepared tomato aspic in a round doughnut mold and a tuna salad marinated in Italian dressing with onions and celery, all on a bed of lettuce. That was one of Jack and Lucien's favorite meals. Allen Ginsberg dropped in so I made some tea and small tuna salad sandwiches for us to nibble on. Allen had iced tea with lemon and mentioned how nice it was and how my tea wasn't like President Butler's tea parties (the President of Columbia), and we snickered.

He started to tell me what he was reading and, as usual, was very animated about it. He recited a long poem from memory, and it was very dramatic the way he did it. He, Jack and Lucien were into Rimbaud and had just started reading the works of Céline. I told Allen how much I appreciated his suggestions and instructions, and how stimulated by our student-teacher relationship I was. When he got up to go he said something that was eerie in light of later events. He described a dream he'd had of an impending disaster in which the four horsemen of the apocalypse rode over the rooftops of Columbia. When he looked out the window, he saw their teeth bared and gleaming and their horsemen's cloaks flying. The image made us both shiver. Allen left and I read Dos Passos while I finished my tea.

At long last Jack came back. He walked over and looked down at me solemnly and without saying a word went in to take a shower. He called out from the bathroom, "Edie, please get me a change of clothes," which I did.

Jack dressed as I started to get our meal ready in the kitchen. I put a cloth over the cocktail table and lit candles. Then I laid out the salad and snacks along with some lemonade I'd just made. Jack had been drinking and was tired, so he stretched out on the couch on top of a clean white sheet that covered it. He said he had some news. He had told the purser that he wouldn't be on his watch that night or the next, so that we could go to the doctor on West End Avenue for our blood tests. "Okay," I said, dumbstruck with astonishment. We had been talking about marriage since I lost the baby, but I wanted to be certain he wasn't doing it out of moral obligation.

We talked a while about our plans to get married. We decided to wait for Joan to come back with her new baby and then take the dog and cat to my mother's in Grosse Pointe. "Couldn't we leave KitKat at your mother's?" I asked him. "No," he said, "There's too much traffic and things like that. It's not good for the cat." After our trip we'd return to New York where I could work in the factories doing war work, which I liked. Jack's allotment check would help pay the rent on the apartment with Joan and we would save whatever we had left to get to Paris after the war.

As I talked about the future, with the classical symphony on the phonograph in the background, Jack fell asleep on the couch. I went over to the mattress on the floor and laid down next to him. We had a shelf for the books our apartment reading club was currently discussing: T.S. Eliot, W.H. Auden, Henry Miller, Jack London and many others. I hadn't yet finished Dos Passos so I picked that up to continue and fell asleep reading.

I didn't wake up until early the next morning and Jack was already making the coffee. He called out, "Rise and shine." Since he was taking the day off he wanted to do something special. I said, "So early?" It was still around 7:00 A.M. He suggested we go see his folks, or go to Asbury Park, or just do something in the city, like cool off in a movie theater. It all sounded great to me, so I dressed quickly as Jack took Woof-it for a walk. In no time he was back and we took the subway to Times Square and went into Bickford's for a breakfast of corned beef hash and eggs. Jack said we'd walk over to the Central Park Zoo and watch them feed the big cats, which we both loved to do. We stayed there for an hour just enjoying the cool shade of the trees.

As we sat on the bus heading home after the blood tests, Jack was unusually quiet. He held my hand tighter than normal. I asked if something was wrong, but he said, "No, nothing. Let's get off at the Thalia and see a movie." As luck would have it, the first show was letting out. The next show started just as we sat down and began munching on our 5th Avenue candy bars. Lowell Thomas came on with a travelogue about India, followed by the Pathe newsreel full of war footage.

The feature happened to be a French movie with English subtitles. I didn't recognize the actors, but Jack did. He and his mother were great French movie fans. They really enjoyed them. I continually asked Jack what they were really saying, and he patiently told me since the dubbing left much to be desired. How he stood all the interruptions of me questioning him while keeping track of what was going on up on the screen, I'll never know, but he did.

When the movie let out I was hungry, so we dropped in for a chicken sandwich and a glass of beer on the way home, which I had to pay for. When I asked him where Lucien was, Jack obviously didn't want to talk about anything he considered gossipy, and we walked back in silence.

Jack was even more quiet than usual. Broadway, late at night, was bursting with people. Even though most of the streetlights were out except at the corners during wartime, I couldn't help but notice that most of the men, whether young or old, were in uniform. Jack was wearing his merchant marine khakis, shirt, pants, black shoes and white socks, and that old beaten up seaman's hat. I was sure proud of him, and it made me feel especially good when other women stared at him hungrily. He never seemed to take notice.

Kingsland had the fan going and was reading Proust on the sofa when we walked in. It was close to midnight by then and a lot cooler. Joan had been trying to get everyone to read Proust so she could discuss his books. John commented that he liked him even though he was dry and difficult to relate to at times. That kind of comment usually got Jack going on long intellectual talks about writing and books, but not tonight. He went into the bathroom for a shower and John left, a bit hurt.

When we went to bed that night, Jack called out for me to lock the door. I was surprised because it was something we never did. After all, who would climb all those stairs? When I went to bed, Jack held out his arms and said, "I want to make love to you—so you will always think of us here and now." I fell into his beauty, never dreaming what very, very real events lay ahead.

chapter 17

. . .

Suddenly I was woken up by a banging on the door, which was a surprise because, as I mentioned, the door was never locked. I called out in my sleep, "The door is open," but it wasn't; I remembered I had locked it. I got up in a daze, wrapped the bath sheet around me and opened the door to find four wild-eyed men there. They came in flashing their badges, saying they were cops. Jack had gotten out of bed when he heard all the noise and was standing in his underwear. One man said, "Get dressed," while another said, "Where's the stash?" I was dumbfounded as they began to search the place, starting with the bathroom. When I had a chance, I put on a cotton checked skirt. As John Kingsland would say, "Really, what does one wear to jail?" I remember I didn't take the police seriously at the time. We didn't have any drugs, plus I knew I had nothing to hide. Jack dressed in his chinos and a white shirt that his mom had washed and ironed. In spite of that, he did look terrible though, really tired. Then I noticed he had handcuffs on, and that's when I got a little scared. Straightaway we all left the apartment. I knocked on the door across the hall and asked Mrs. McCorkle to mind the animals. Then we went down the stairs; one cop in front, one with me, and two with Jack, one handcuffed to him. They had street suits on so I assumed they were detectives.

There were two squad cars with their lights flashing parked in the middle of the street, so traffic could not get by. They put us in separate cars so we couldn't talk to each other. Then, as I sat in the squad car, Kingsland walked past and spotted us. When we didn't acknowledge him, he knew something was up. The cops drove us directly to the 100th Street precinct stationhouse. They took Jack and me up some stairs to separate glass-enclosed offices. One detective asked if I wanted coffee. "Yes, please," I said politely, wanting them to know that I was a proper young lady. A tough-looking cop came in and said, "You turn tricks and that guy's your pimp." I gasped with shock. The other cop with angel eyes said, "Come on, Bob, anyone can see she's a nice young lady with a Detroit driver's license. We'll call and see if there are any tickets or anything else."

After I finished my coffee I asked them what it was all about, thinking that my mother or grandmother had reported our apartment as being a den of iniquity. These burly guys must have decided to take it seriously. Then the officer in charge said, "That pal of yours, Lucien, knocked off his lover." I gasped and asked, "Is Celine dead?" I was horrified, but I also felt like laughing, it seemed so preposterous. Next, I almost broke down into tears, "My God! What happened?" I quickly realized they were not going to tell me. I had to sit on that hard wooden chair with two sadistic cops who would tell me nothing about my friend's death. Then I became angry and went into my routine, "Do you know who I am? Where I come from? Who my family are?" Of course, they could have cared less, and they looked at me as if I were crazy. Then the one with angel eyes said, "Your boyfriend's in there spilling his guts out . . . so why don't you confess?"

"To what?" I responded, "He's my fiancée!" "Since when, three minutes ago?" he said sarcastically. After a while I was taken into a carpeted, wood-paneled office. It looked just like something a big shot lawyer would have. There was a man who looked like Groucho Marx sitting behind a huge desk with a sign on it that read "Jacob Grumet, Ass't. District Attorney."

"Well, your boyfriend has confessed," Grumet told me. "To what?" I replied. No answer.

"So you're this kid's mistress. He tells me you're living together." "Yes," I said, "for over two years now. We have our blood test certificate and we planned to be married before he shipped out." With that I produced the blood test papers.

He looked at them and said, "So, we have a 'love nest' going on up on 118th Street with orgies all the time." By then I thought the whole world was nuts. Then came a silly statement, "I bet you're pregnant." I was going to deny it, but I felt this might help me get out of this unreal situation so I didn't. "Uh-huh. I knew there was something going on," he said. Then he began, "This queer, Lucien Carr . . ." I interrupted, "Lucien is not queer, he likes girls, and especially Celine. They are, or were, in love." I still believed she was dead.

"What do you mean, were?" he said. "Did they split up? A lover's spat, perhaps?" I was beginning to wonder when this nightmare was going to end. Then the D.A. asked, "Are you going to talk?" "Why, yes, of course," I said, "but about what?" He got up and called the policeman, who took me into another glass room. I could see Jack going into Grumet's office next. I sat down and the police resumed their interrogation. "Tell me about your boyfriend." "Like what?" I asked.

"Like what kind of funny cigarettes does he smoke?" "Lucky Strikes," I quickly answered. He didn't laugh.

"Does he like boys?" he asked. I said, "Are you nuts? Do I look like a boy to you?" as I stuck my chest out. He gazed with appreciation out of his little pig eyes.

"Tell me what happened to you last Sunday night," he said. I told him we had taken the subway downtown. "Who did you meet there?"

"Well, no one in particular. We went to a show in the Village." He wanted to know who was with us. "Lucien and his girl, Celine, Jack and myself, and oh yes, Bill, Bill Burroughs."

"The adding machine guy?" he asked. I didn't bother to answer that one. "We went to a Chinese restaurant then took the subway home."

"What time was that, about 10:00?"

"Oh, by then Bill wasn't with us. Celine, Lucien, Jack and I stopped at the West End and joined a few friends."

"Like who?" he asked.

"Just friends," I answered.

"Was Dave Kammerer there?" he wanted to know.

"No! Well, he did come in later and sat by himself at the bar."

"Why was that?" he continued, more interested now.

"He's a pest and I can't stand him. But he left right away. We stayed and had a couple of beers, then we all left. Lucien walked Celine to the subway while Jack and I went back to our apartment."

"Did you see Celine go into the subway for home?" he asked.

"No, but I know Lucien always stayed with her until she got on the train. He is very much a gentleman," I assured him. I was trying to score some points for Lucien if I could. At this stage of the game I could tell Lucien was in trouble. Since they were trying to find out about Celine, I kept thinking something had happened to her and that Lucien was at fault. Could that be true?

One officer left the room and another came in to question me further. In a quiet voice he asked if Lucien was very involved with Celine. I said yes and added that he seemed to care for no other. "How well do you know him?" the man asked.

"Very well! He's very close to both me and Jack." I was hoping he didn't think we were romantically involved. "He's at our apartment a lot. We take the same art class, so we paint together doing our homework."

"What does your boyfriend think of that?" he persisted.

"He's usually there," I answered.

"Otherwise he wouldn't trust you with this Lucien kid?" he twisted it.

"No, that's not it at all," I said, getting flustered and playing into his hands.

Then he said, "I see you're pregnant. Could Lucien have had anything to do with that?"

"No! That's crazy—I love Jack and he loves me," I stated flatly.

"Now tell me more about Sunday night and Monday," he continued.

"Well, Jack and I left Lucien and Celine at the subway entrance and went home to walk our dog. We walked to Morningside Drive to let her run in the park and sat on a bench while Jack had his goodnight smoke, Lucky Strike," I added quickly. "Then David Kammerer came up the street looking for Lucien. We told him he had taken Celine home—letting him think he had. He's a real pest."

"What do you mean pest?" his eyes lit up.

"He's always around where he is not wanted," I answered honestly.

"Who doesn't want him?" he pressed further.

"All of us except Bill. Dave's his friend from St. Louis. They are much older than we are, and Lucien and Celine are two years younger than Jack and me. Bill and Dave are eight years older," I added without being asked.

"What was Dave's frame of mind when you saw him that night?"

"The same as always. Anxious, wringing his sweaty hands, hurrying to us then racing away. No one likes him," I stated. "He's a real pest and not welcome in my apartment."

"Why not?" asked the cop.

"Well, he tried to harm our cat once," I explained.

"Really? How?"

"Well, I wasn't there, and I don't think Dave is all there either," I suggested. Then the policeman asked me to tell him about it. At this point the cop asked me to call him by his first name, in a flirtatious way that I didn't appreciate. "Dave tried to hang our cat by its neck with his tie. I believe he really meant to do it, but Bill stopped him. I think that's a very childish thing to do, him being thirty-three years old," I said.

"How did you know how old he was?" I did not bother to answer that one.

I had no idea what had happened, they had me believing that something had happened to Celine. I was beginning to think that Dave had probably done her harm. It was a terrible feeling. Then that officer left the room and went into Grumet's office.

Before long he came out, walked over to me and said I could go. "Can I please see Jack?" I asked. By that time Jack was nowhere in sight and I couldn't see into Grumet's office. I said I wouldn't go anywhere until I could see my fiancée, but they said, "He's at the Bronx jail being processed."

"What does that mean?" I asked, hoping they'd tell me what he was being charged with.

"Fingerprinted . . . picture taken . . . put on the wire, etcetera. Then he goes to court tomorrow morning for the arraignment."

"What does that all mean?" I asked again, but no answer.

STUDENT IS SILENT ON SLAYING FRIEND

Held Without Bail After He Listens Lackadaisically to Charge in Stabbing Case

Clasping a copy of "A Vision," a philosophical work by W. B. Yeats, under one arm, Lucien Carr, 19-year-old Columbia sophomore, listened lackadaisically to the proceeding as he was arraigned yesterday morning before Magistrate Anna M. Kross in Homicide Court. He was held without bail for a hearing on Aug. 29.

The pale, slender youth showed little interest as Detective James O'Brien presented a short affidavit charging him with homicide for having faitfully stabbed on Monday David Kammerer, 33-year-old former instructor at Washington University, St. Louis, with whom he had been friendly. His attorney, Vincent J. Malone, told the court that the defendant had nothing to say.

Court Asks Psychiatric Test

Magistrate Kross asked Mr. Malone whether he had any objection to having Carr sent to Bellevue Hospital for psychiatric observation at this time. Mr. Malone replied that he did object and would prefer to have the case follow the usual channels. Jacob Grumet, assistant district attorney in charge of the Homicide Bureau, also objected to the proposal, saying that that should be done in the Court of General Sessions.

Exclaiming that "we in the great State of New York still proceed under the early theory of eighteenth century justice," Magistrate Kross declared that this procedure would result in "a great loss of time." She said that the procedure she had suggested would be valuable in

Lucien Carr as he was arraigned yesterday.   The New York Times.

day. Appearing greatly concerned at the high bail set, he pleaded with Judge Sullivan to reduce it to a point that his parents, who live in Ozone Park, Queens, might be able to meet.

"They'll take very good care of you in the new city prison," Judge Sullivan assured him as he was led away.

Kammerer's Parents Prominent
Special to The New York Times.

ST. LOUIS, Aug. 16—David Kammerer was the son of socially prominent Mr. and Mrs. Alfred L. Kammerer of Clayton, Mo., a suburb of St. Louis. His father is a consulting engineer. The son was graduated from John Burroughs School here in 1929 and from Washington University in 1933.

After some teaching experience he returned to the university and obtained a Master's degree in 1938. He specialized in English and for a time was an instructor in that subject and in physical education. His father said that he had done some study toward a doctorate at Columbia, but recently had been tutoring and was not connected with that institution.

Mr. Kammerer said that he had received a letter from his son last week in which he wrote of a pleasant meeting with Lucien Carr, a friend he had known for some time.

David Eames Kammerer

Columbia Student Kills Friend And Sinks Body in Hudson River

By FRANK S. ADAMS

A fantastic story of a homicide, first revealed to the authorities by the voluntary confession of a 19-year-old Columbia sophomore, was converted yesterday from a nightmarish fantasy into a horrible reality by the discovery of the bound and stabbed body of the victim in the murky waters of the Hudson River.

For twenty-four hours previously the police and the district attorney's office, balked by the absence of a body or a particle of evidence corroborating the commission of any crime, had detained the self-proclaimed slayer without a charge. He stayed in the district attorney's office, peacefully reading poetry most of the night.

But with the discovery of the body yesterday afternoon, which the slender, studious youth unshakingly identified as it was lifted from the water, and after he had led detectives to the spot where he had buried his victim's eye glasses in Morningside Park, the investigators knew that they were dealing with a real homicide and not the imaginings of an overstrained mind.

Lucien Carr, 19 years old, son of a family formerly prominent in St. Louis, but now living in this city, was the youth who admitted the killing. The authorities said that he was the son of Russell Carr

Continued on Page 13

chapter 18

· · ·

I was so shaken, I stumbled out and went down the stairs to the street. Once I got to the apartment, I found Celine sitting on the couch, coolly sipping iced tea. I sat down. I was speechless and burst into tears. "What's wrong?" she asked.

"I thought you were hurt, or worse, dead. And that Kammerer had done it." I told her all I knew, which was very little. "Jack and Lucien need a lawyer, do you know any?" Celine asked me.

"Well, Gram's lawyer is working on grandfather's estate.* He's a friend of ours, so I'll call him and see. Let's do it right now." So we headed for the phone booths near the Lion's Den on campus. People we knew were acting funny, so I finally asked someone what was going on? He said, "Get a newspaper."

---

* Edie's grandfather, Walter Mackay Parker had died on June 4, 1942.

We ran across Broadway to the newsstand and bought a *Tribune* and a *Daily News*. The headline in the *News* read, "HONOR SLAYER—COLUMBIA STUDENT MURDERS LOVER." Then at the very end it said, "over his girlfriend, a love triangle." It was the same in the *Tribune*, but there they mentioned Jack as an "accessory." Also that his mistress had been questioned but not detained. It said that Jack and Lucien were being held in the Bronx jail on $5,000 bond. Celine and I were devastated and she figured we better hide out immediately. We ran back to the apartment, collected the dog and cat, locked up the apartment and took a cab to Kingsland's apartment in Brooklyn Heights.

When we got to John's he came out paid the cab, and then helped us with our things. His mother was teaching and his dad was off at work in City Hall, so we gathered in a sunroom that overlooked a small, lovely flower garden. Very English, I thought. The first thing we did was call Joan. She had heard the news on the radio and was shocked that anyone would believe Lucien "liked men" in any way, shape or form. She was very optimistic that things would work themselves out.

Then we wondered what to do about raising the bail money. I suggested Lucien's family perhaps, or Burroughs, but $5,000 was a lot of money. Jack's father was so angry with Jack that he told him that no Kerouac had ever gotten involved in anything like that and he was on his own.

After talking to Joan I called our lawyer, Herbert Kennedy, and we had a long conversation. He asked me detailed questions about Jack, the murder, and our relationship. I was very embarrassed about admitting we lived together and I'm afraid I made it sound a little like a lark I was having, which was far from the truth. I could not have been more emphatic about feeling responsible for Jack, however. It was I who had introduced him to Lucien, for Lucien had originally been my friend first. If it weren't for me, he wouldn't be in this mess. Right away the lawyer warned me, "You know this is all going to cost, Edith."

"Well," I said, "my inheritance from grandfather is being probated and I will sign over anything to get Jack out of jail." Then I started to fall apart. I told him we were planning to marry, "I have the blood test here in my purse, we love each other." I began to cry.

"I'll call Judge Manuel C. Avin to see if you can borrow on your inheritance. Everything is tied up in probate court back in Detroit. I'll call you back later. In the meantime, I'll call the proper authorities and get everything in motion. I don't know how much of the inheritance is for you; your grandfather's assets are still being liquidated. I'm sure there is enough to take care of Mr. Kerouac, though, if the judge will permit it," he added. I hung up wondering which judge he meant. The probate judge or Jack's?

We piled into John's mother's car and took off for Pelham, up in Westchester, where Celine lived. From there I called Kennedy again. He said Judge G.L. Donnellan was a friend of his and that the judge was planning to reduce Jack's bail the next day, seeing that Jack was so well connected. The evidence was all in and he had determined that Jack was not an "accessory to murder" but a misguided seaman with the circumstances against him. In other words, Lucien was the villain, not Jack. Jack had just followed him.

Then I said, "You know, Mr. Kennedy, Lucien is a nice guy.

I'm sure it's as the paper says, self-defense. His girl is sitting right next to me and we both know he only likes women."

Then Kennedy said, "She better call District Attorney Grumet. She's wanted for questioning." He told us that the police were just beginning to think about getting a warrant out for her and this "joy boy" John Kingsland. "Now listen, Edith," he said, "I'm afraid the probate judge has some bad news for you. You will have to marry Jack before we can pay his bond."

"How in the world can I do that?" I asked.

"The judge and I will arrange it as soon as possible. We don't want your fiancée in jail, do we? You do have the blood test?" he asked.

"Yes!" I assured him.

"You must have the Young girl call up Grumet immediately," he reminded me.

"Can I see Jack?" I begged.

"I'll arrange it," he said, and with that he hung up and I relayed his message to Celine.

We just sat there in silence for a while, both lost in the gloom of the world which had enveloped us. She called Grumet and he told her to come to his office to give a statement the following morning. He also said that although I could see Jack, Celine could not see Lucien. "It will be a long time before anyone sees that boy," Grumet informed her. Celine's face turned white.

I knew Lucien's lawyer was Kenneth Spence, and Celine and I debated whether we should call him or not. We dialed his number and his receptionist put us through. Spence advised me to not discuss the case with anyone and then spoke to Celine at greater length. When she hung up she started to sob again. He had also told Celine that it would be a long time before she, or anyone except his family, could see Lucien. We would both be called as witnesses and should expect it was going to be terrible. When Celine's mother came in, she was carrying the newspaper. There were no headlines this time, but the story was still on the front page under the heading, "Honor Slaying." Lucien was to be arraigned for first degree murder and we could barely believe what we were reading. They described Jack as "an ex-football hero" mentioning a few of his exploits on the gridiron. He was going to be arraigned as an "accessory after the fact," it said, for helping Lucien dispose of the murder weapon and Kammerer's eyeglasses. They also mentioned that they were both merchant seamen, which would have pleased Lucien under different circumstances. The article went on about Lucien coming from St. Louis with Dave, who had been his Boy Scout troop leader, now age thirty-five to Lucien's nineteen.

Celine's mother was wonderful. She started to make dinner for us while Celine and I talked about what we would bring Jack. He needed something to read, but as we wondered what, Joan called again suggesting we take an assortment: Rimbaud, Keats, Butler, Huxley, and Maugham, the latter being one of Joan's favorites along with Proust. So before we went downtown the next day we needed to slip into the apartment and pick up the books. That night we went to bed early. I read Rose Franklyn, very light reading, but I couldn't read long because I was so beat and tired.

chapter 19

. . .

The next morning, Wednesday, August 16, we spoke to Kingsland, who was being called in for questioning along with
Ginsberg. I suppose everyone who knew Lucien was being
asked. We told John we'd see him at the police station. Celine
and I felt miserable. Both our men were in jail, hers quite possibly for good. Mine? Who knew? We took a commuter line
to the city and then the subway to Columbia. We wanted to
avoid seeing anyone on campus so we sneaked up the back
stairs. There were several notes on the door, but I cautioned
Celine, "Don't touch them. They're probably from the papers."
I got the books for Jack and a change of clothes, his shaving
equipment and a toothbrush. He must be going nuts not being
able to brush his teeth, I thought. Jack had a fetish for brushing his teeth. Celine and I put everything in brown grocery
bags and slipped out the same way we came in, through the

laundry room. Before going into the 100th Street precinct, I stopped and bought six packs of Lucky's for Jack. It seemed that in all the jailhouse movies I had seen, the inmates were always bumming cigarettes. We walked up the worn stone steps to the detective bureau on the second floor. There I asked for Grumet, but now I didn't know if he was a detective or an assistant district attorney, or what, so I just said, Grumet. I told the officers that Miss Young and Miss Parker were there to visit an inmate. God, how gruesome it sounded, an inmate! They announced on the intercom, "Detective James O'Brien, visitor for case number 58611-14." Jesus! Jack already had a prison number! It was getting worse by the minute. Then one of the policemen from before came, and I told him I was staying at Miss Young's. "That's good. We're talking to Mr. Ginsberg and Mr. Kingsland now," he told us. I looked, but they were nowhere to be seen. We got on the Lysol-scented elevator and went up two floors. It was very noisy as we went through a steel bar door that banged shut behind us. Lucien was coming down a small corridor handcuffed to a detective. I didn't recognize him at first. He looked terrible; still in the same dirty clothes. We spoke briefly and I told him that Celine and I were staying together at her house. I handed him the first three books and noticed that he was visibly shaken. He looked at them and said, "These are library books. I'll have to take them back or pay the fine." Then he gave me a weak smile as he was pulled away by the detective. That was the last time I would see Lucien again for several years. Allen was right when he said, "The libertine circle is destroyed."

The detective and I turned a corner of the steel corridor and came to a cell. There was my poor Jack, looking as dirty as

Lucien, sporting a two day stubble on his face. He scratched his head as he approached the bars of his cell. He put his hands through the bars and took all the stuff I had brought and said, "Thanks! Man, oh, man! Do I need smokes!" The detective left us alone briefly. Me on the outside wanting to get in; Jack on the inside wanting to get out. I told him about the lawyer, the probate judge, and what they had said.

"What does it matter? We'll just get married by a justice of the peace or something." I think he was suspicious that I, or my family, had arranged the marriage set-up, but I certainly had not. I told him, "These lawyers and judges are very straight and unbending, I think they have a power complex. I just saw poor Lucien. Thank God for his family or he would fry for sure." Jack shook his head in agreement.

"You'll go up before the judge today or tomorrow," I explained.

"Boy, they don't fool around, do they?" he said. He told me there was a Negro there who sang the blues like Leadbelly, really gut feeling, beautiful music. "I wish you could hear him," he said. We were holding hands through the thick bars when the detective came back and said, "Time." Jack threw me a kiss as I was ushered away. I forgot to tell him about Celine being questioned, but he might have guessed. He had all the newspapers folded on his bunk on top of a scratchy army blanket. The officer said Jack would be transferred to the Bronx jail before the weekend, so I volunteered, "We plan on getting married very soon. Can he do that in jail?" He really didn't know about that.

"I have our blood test right here," and motioned to my purse.

"First, you have to get your marriage license at the Municipal Building on Chambers Street, then you can talk to the judge's clerk. Maybe she can figure something out," he said. I could tell he didn't think Jack would be getting out anytime soon and was just humoring me, although he did realize the urgency of the situation and seemed to care. He walked me down some stairs where I could see they were talking to Allen and John. They had finished with Celine, who was sitting waiting for me on one of the steel folding chairs. As I approached I could see she'd been crying. I gave the policeman one of those "fuck you" stares as he walked me over to her. I could see his eyes light up as we approached Celine, a gorgeous, athletic blonde. Funny, when a girl is your friend you never look at them the same way a man does, at least I don't.

Celine went with me to Chambers Street to get the marriage license application. In the Municipal Building an old elevator took us up to the second floor where we got in a small line at a cage of sorts, like tellers have at a bank. I remember the sign clearly, "City Clerk, N. Warren Huffaith, Borough of Manhattan." The clerk handed me an application and said it had to be filled out and returned within six days. After that we had twenty-four hours to be married, or was it the other way around? I was so nervous I could hardly remember. Then the clerk asked, "Where is the groom? It's customary for both of you to fill it out here."

"Well, he's on a ship in port," I was quick to reply. I grabbed the damn thing and raced for the exit.

In the elevator, Celine was laughing, "Well, you better be sure this is what you want." Just imagine, the perennial "virgin," laughing at me. I felt I had practically been horsewhipped by the cops, nearly thrown in the slammer, but this marriage stuff was too much. "Well," I suggested, "let's have a drink." We headed for a bar nearby, where I ordered rum and coke. That was the only hard liquor they had. I noticed I was shaking, that's how nervous I was. Celine was a little more sympathetic so I managed to calm down.

After the drink we went back to Pelham, and once there the phone began to ring. It was the newspaper reporters asking for the future Mrs. Kerouac. I guess the detective couldn't keep his trap shut, not only about Pelham, but about Celine and me staying there, too. I was starting to worry about what Sister and Gram would think of all this. I knew they were in Asbury Park, but I hoped at least Gram's friends wouldn't recognize me as the future Mrs. Kerouac, one small blessing. The *Daily Mirror* was the only paper to still have the "Honor Slaying" on the front page by then. The others had moved it to the back or dropped it altogether. The *Mirror* was the only one to mention the "New Vision" that Allen was forever spouting about, so I knew they had talked to him. I remember thinking that he wasn't helping Lucien by leading them to think we were all political radicals by talking about philosophy. I wondered why they would print that stuff anyway? It sounded like Allen was quoting some textbook he was reading, or Dostoyevsky's *Crime and Punishment* or perhaps Nietzsche. Allen and Jack were always engaged in some kind of verbal battle about the way the world was, and how it got that way. To a girl like me, it was a very inactive way of having fun, but they enjoyed arguing about things they couldn't change. It was a never-ending discussion, about one author after another, exhausting one subject or writer only to jump to another that was coming from a new direction.

One of the phone calls was from our lawyer, Herbert Kennedy, telling me that they were going to arraign Jack the next morning at ten. He would be there, and directed me not to come. He would do all he could to reduce the charges and lower his bond. I asked him what Jack's chances were, but he wouldn't commit himself and reminded us to stay away from the newspapers. He also said that there would probably be a jury trial and that any public comments we might make would lower their chances.

As soon as I hung up the phone, it rang again. This time it was Jack's mother, Gabe. I informed her of what was happening. She was very grateful that I had gotten a lawyer for her "Jackie." She told me that Leo, Jack's father, was so upset he wouldn't talk about it, much less help Jack. "Leo says he can rot in jail with his highfalutin' friend. Let *him* help him," Gabe told me. I didn't tell her of the marriage license, or the terms Kennedy had put down. What was the use? She would no doubt side with Leo. Jack's parents liked me and knew we had been living together for two years, but I doubt if they thought of me as good marriage material for their precious son, Jack. Heaven knows, my family felt the same way.

Celine and I called John Kingsland and told him about the court date, and he said he would go. His family had warned him to stay away from his bohemian friends, but wild horses couldn't have done that, knowing John. He said he would call Joan, too.

chapter 20

Thursday morning we got up late. Celine and I went down to
the kitchen for breakfast with her mother. I couldn't get over
the food. Where did they find eggs and fresh bread? It was so
hard to get. Even sugar was tightly rationed, and there was no
substitute for it then. You needed a special ration book for
sugar alone during the war. The same was true for shoes.

Well, we both sat there feeling gloomy. It's surprising that
we never really discussed what had happened with Lucien and
Dave. We just went on with our lives. I recall wondering how
a man like Dave Kammerer, who was unwanted by most people, could be in New York City for such a short period of time
and raise such havoc. He not only looked like the devil, but
acted like him as well.

I was startled out of my thoughts by the ringing of the
phone. This time it was Celine's handsome brother, Phil,

calling from Princeton where he was in training to be an officer in the army. He had been reading about everything in the newspapers and called to ask if she wanted him home to help. "No, Edie is here and mom is taking it fine," Celine assured him. When she hung up, I could see what all of this was doing to poor Celine for the first time. She was in love with someone who was taken away from her, not knowing if or when she would ever see him again. She had dark circles under her eyes from lack of sleep. I got her some coffee, trying to cheer her up and said, "Celine, he'll beat this. You know Lucien!"

Celine and I made clothes to kill time. She didn't know how to sew very well, so I taught her how to use her mother's sewing machine. Celine made clothes while I worked on curtains for the apartment. The time passed more quickly as we worked at our projects. We got the *Herald Tribune* that morning and were happy to find no mention of the case. At least the papers were finished with us. It was old news now. Then I called the super at our apartment and asked him to take in the mail. Luckily, I got him and he said, "Fine." I could hear his wife in the background asking, "Are they going to move? Ask her, Gus," but he didn't.

The phone rang again; this time it was Herbert Kennedy's secretary. She was very curt and informed me, "Mr. Kerouac's charge of accessory after the fact has been changed to material witness with the bail bond reduced from $5,000 to $2,500. Mr. Kennedy is arranging for you to visit Mr. Kerouac in the Bronx Jail when he's transferred. He is also getting in touch with a bail bondsman for you and will call you later on that other matter. Thank you." Down went the receiver.

I decided I would go and see Jack as soon as I could in the Bronx. He had to fill out the marriage license application so I could turn it in. I got ready to go alone, quickly. "If Kennedy calls, tell him I'll be home by five; fill him in on what I'm doing," I told Celine. It was raining hard when I got to the Grand Concourse subway stop. I stood under a barbershop awning and decided I'd better try to hail a cab, especially since I didn't know exactly where I was going. It took a while because of the weather, but I got one and the cabby took me about a mile and a half to the jail. I got out, paid the fare and went into a five-story stone building with peepholes for windows. It was chilly when I first went inside, as the rain had cooled everything off. The desk sergeant directed me to a large visiting room where they would bring Jack for fifteen minutes. Wow! What were we doing here, Jack and me, I asked myself? I couldn't believe all this was happening. I sat down at a caged wall with chairs on both sides, waiting. There was one other woman there also waiting for her man.

When they brought Jack in he sat down opposite me, with the glass between us and a hole to speak through. He looked clean, but needed a haircut. He also looked very pale. I could hardly hold back my tears as he tried to smile and asked how everything was going. "Well," I said, "Celine and I are comforting each other in Pelham. I've talked to your mother. She seems to be more upset with Leo than with what you are going through. I tell her what little I know. Here are the marriage forms to fill out. You do it, then I will. Okay?"

"What have you heard from Bill or Lucien?" he asked. Burroughs was arrested too, because Lucien went and told him everything before he turned himself in. That made him an accessory. His family got him out and made him go back to St. Louis until he had to testify in court.

"Nothing," I said. Then I told him I thought Kingsland had said Bill would be leaving town pretty quickly. "Maybe Bill has left town already, I really don't know," I said. I felt better not telling him anything. I really didn't care about it now that Jack's bail would be paid.

"They questioned everybody, I understand. I'm sure they told them the same as you; that Lucien likes girls," he suggested.

Anyway, I hadn't heard from Bill or Allen and no one could talk to Lucien. Jack gave me a letter for the Maritime Union explaining what happened to make sure he wasn't considered to be absent without leave. I asked if he wanted me to call, but he said no, the letter was better. Later, I did ask Grumet to call them, just to make it official. Jack said, "There are a lot of very strange types in here—prisoners."

"Like what?" I asked, but I really didn't want to know.

"Well, they're all hostile. I think because I have books they think I'm a stoolie. A guy said if I came near him, he'd clean my clock. They are very frightened of me and give me a wide berth."

Fifteen minutes were up far too soon. The guard let us have a few seconds longer, but finally he got up and said, "Time's up," and Jack and the other prisoner walked out together. I heard him say, "How's it going?" to Jack. Jack just said a flat, "Fine." The lady and I went out together, but we never spoke. She got in a limo, which was very rare in those gas-rationing times, and I walked to the subway, deep in my own thoughts. At least the rain had stopped.

When I caught the next train for Pelham it was crowded with commuters and everyone in the club car was drinking. A salesman bought me a martini with an olive. Olives were very hard to get, but the railroad had booze and olives even when no one else could get them. Probably they had stockpiled them before the war got so bad. Some people took the New Rochelle train just to have two drinks, then got off at 125th Street and took the subway back into the city. It was a great way to beat the hassle of the packed subway, plus have a drink with free peanuts. Sitting in the club car took my mind off Jack until the salesman asked me what I was up to. I admitted that I had been visiting my con boyfriend in the slammer. He moved away, terror showing in his suburban eyes. I got off in Pelham and took a bus to Celine's.

When I got back, Celine, her mother and I had tea and cookies in the living room. I told them of my visit with Jack, and they told me that the D.A.'s office had called, but not Grumet. We were to stay in easy reach and should expect to be called as character witnesses at the trial. I asked if Lucien's charges had been reduced from first degree murder, but they said no, nothing had changed.

chapter 21

. . .

The next day I woke up feeling much older; so much had happened in only one week. All of our lives had changed, drastically, all because of Dave, who Lucien had tried to avoid, just as we all did. Kammerer had been like a puppet on the end of marionette strings being manipulated by the wind. He wanted the unattainable, Lucien. We had all tried to be kind to him, but he was a person possessed by his own selfish ego. To hell with anything or anyone else, even Lucien. We all tried to talk sense into him about Lucien and Celine, but he believed only what he wanted to believe.

I went into our apartment early and collected my letters from the mailbox. I read all of the messages and then tossed them into the garbage. Allen had written something about having been around to see me, but his handwriting was too difficult for me to read. There was a letter from Gram and Sis in Asbury, too, with no mention of the crime, and no mention of Jack either, thank God!

I had packed most of our things in boxes and shoved them nearer the front door so the express man could gather them more easily when the time came to leave. We had paid the rent through August and weren't planning to renew the lease since we needed more space. By ten I was at the jail again. They ushered me into the same room as before. I had picked up some razors, since Jack shaved twice a day, and handed him the package, but the guard grabbed it first, looked inside and then handed it back to Jack. I tried to be casual, "What have you been up to?" He told me he had gone to Bellevue Hospital to identify Kammerer in the morgue.

"My gosh! That's terrible. Couldn't they have gotten Burroughs or Kingsland to do it?" I asked.

"I guess not," he said and smiled on the side of his mouth. "They've been playing poker near me in a well-known gangster's cell, it goes on all the time. I can hear them but I can't see them," he said.

"Where are you?"

"On the fourth floor," he answered. I handed him some money, not very much, for I had very little, but he needed it for laundry and cigarettes. Jack and I held hands under the small barred window for a minute. We both transmitted our love and sympathy to each other quietly. Then Jack was tapped lightly on the shoulder with the guard's nightstick, the fifteen minutes were up and he had to go back to his cell. "Take care of Woof-it, KitKat and yourself," he said. "I'll see you Monday. No visiting over the weekend." I walked away slowly, feeling as if I was in a movie, hoping the lights would go on and the nightmare would end.

We were still waiting to hear from the judge about when and where they could marry us. Since it was the weekend, we probably couldn't get married until Monday or Tuesday at the earliest. I called Judge Murray W. Stand as soon as I got back to Celine's and arranged it. Our license had been approved, so the three-day waiting period, with the weekend added on meant it would no doubt be Tuesday before we'd be married. I wished Joan could have been there to be my maid of honor, but Celine was willing. Jack didn't really like Celine that much, but I did. Jack thought she was immature. The virginal act she handed out was too much for a real man, which Jack was, at least to me. Celine was Lucien's age, nineteen to our twenty-one.

This time, going back to Pelham in the early afternoon, there was no open club car. So I sat alone with my very gloomy thoughts in a Pullman car. The house was empty when I arrived. Gabe called and I told her all about her son, but left out the part about our getting married. She said she still wasn't talking to Leo yet. Actually, that made me chuckle because it was exactly what he would have liked, no conversation at all. A half-hour later, John Kingsland called. We talked about the case and Jack and me getting married. He asked if he could help in any way, but there wasn't much he could do. There were really no definite plans yet, it was all impromptu and depended upon the police. John was supportive and said he was sorry I was going to marry Jack. "I always hoped we could have a fling together," he said. John had wanted us to be more than friends since we first met when he came over to the apartment with Lucien and

Mary Moran, Lucien's girl at the time. He and Lucien were classmates and Mary, who was also from St. Louis, was going to art school in Philadelphia.

Not long after I spoke with John, Celine raced in and then her mother. We started to gab about the wedding and what I would wear. Having someone like Celine to talk to made me more enthusiastic about it. My cousin from Chicago was a part-time buyer at Best & Company, and she had a lot of clout at Best's. I suggested that Celine and I could go there and pick out my outfit. I said to Celine, "I wonder where Bill is? I guess he went back to St. Louis, and who could blame him? Who wants to get mixed up with the law anyway? They sure don't give a damn who the hell you are, do they?"

Mrs. Young was cooking a meatloaf and it smelled delicious. Celine mixed up a salad while I set the table in the dining room. After dinner Celine's brother, Phil, had a couple of buddies over to the house. They were both on leave from the Marine Corps and had been in the South Pacific with General MacArthur. One had even been an aide of MacArthur. They made me think of my brother, Bill. I hoped he would never get wind of the unfortunate tragedy that had befallen Jack and me. He knew from my last letter that we were definitely getting married.

chapter 22

· · ·

The next morning the weather was not as hot as it had been, but terribly windy. We got to Best & Company right after they opened and went up to find my cousin, Patsy. She was truly gorgeous, the first woman I knew who wore her hair short, only an inch and a half long, with dark black curls all over her head. Patsy was beaming and extremely happy for me about my impending marriage. She said she had just the outfit, "Not too dressy and great for a jailhouse wedding." We all giggled at that. She brought a Paris creation out of the back room that was not even on display yet. I tried it on. It had a creamy white top, large dolman sleeves nipped in at the wrists with tiny buttons down the front. It fit tight at the waist and then flared out to a peplum. The skirt was black and semi-full, stopping just below the knees. It had a low neckline but you could button it up as high as you wanted to. I must say I've never looked as good in an outfit again. We picked out a pair of high-heeled shoes and an envelope-type tan purse to match. The bill came to $125, which I charged to Gram. We both had the same names and that's all you needed back then, there were no charge plates. Cash, check or your signature, that was it, they never even looked at your driver's license.

Celine already had a white dress she could wear that seemed appropriate. We both were going to wear short veils with flowers sewn sparingly through them. On the first floor we bought some tiny silk rose buds with green leaves for a bridal bouquet. I believe these were the last of the Japanese-made imports. When those were gone—zip! There would be no more. With all our packages, we swung over to Schraftt's for lunch. It was a typically crowded Saturday. We had coffee and tea sandwiches, and while we indulged in a hot caramel sundae for dessert, a little boy of seven was sent over to our table to ask for my autograph. He said, "Can I have your signature on my school book, Miss Stanwyck?" That happened to me a lot, so I exaggerated my handwriting and wrote "Barbara Stinkwick." Celine and I could barely control our laughter.

We walked towards Times Square, and since we had a couple of hours to kill before going to Kingsland's in Brooklyn, I suggested a movie. "Great," Celine said. We had seen *Grand Illusion* at least three times, so we went to see Hedy Lamarr in *Ecstasy*. Jack would never have gone to see it, scandalous in it's day for the nude scenes. It was dumb, with Hedy continually hiding behind a bush with some guy looking at her, it was just stupid.

After the show we caught the subway to Brooklyn, where John lived in a large brownstone-type house filled with dark furniture and wall to wall carpeting. The shades were usually drawn and the drapes pulled shut so it was always cool inside. John greeted us wearing a white, short sleeve shirt with an ascot and smoking a cigarette in a holder. A lot of people did this because the cigarettes tasted terrible. The tobacco companies used a very poor grade of tobacco for civilian consumption. That's the reason everyone clamored for servicemen's cigarettes. "Come on, let's go sit in the conservatory," John invited, "it's cool there." With John, you felt you had just stepped onto a Hollywood set. We sat there on cushioned, black wicker chairs with a ceiling fan overhead and water trickling in the fishpond—it was idyllic.

"What can I get you? I can make gin squashes with lime," he offered. Celine and I agreed that sounded good. John went to the kitchen and brought back a silver tray gleaming with chilled crystal cocktail glasses and a pitcher of lime juice over crushed ice. He filled the glasses, stuck short straws in them, and handed each of us a glass with a black linen doily. I commented that it was too bad he and Bill didn't see eye to eye, for Burroughs would love the setting—he would say it was "Casbah-ish." The only thing missing was Sydney Greenstreet.

John was pleased, his party was a success. I made a hamper of chicken and hors d'oeuvres to go with a picnic dinner while John chilled two bottles of wine. "I thought we could go to Swan Lake in Prospect Park," John said. It was his nature to always be the courting swan. That was why Joan loved him so; he did everything with a dramatic flair. Off we went with hampers, glasses and blankets—"the works." You would never have known that death and murder wore heavy on our minds. We spread two blankets out on the grassy slope overlooking the swans and a bridle path. John opened the chilled bottle of Asti Spumante and poured some into our crystal glasses, then made a toast, "Here's to better times."

"Yeah! Yeah!" Celine and I chirped. John put his glass down and rubbed his hands together. Both he and Jack had the same habit of doing that whenever they were about to say something they had given a lot of thought to. "What are these wedding plans of yours?" he asked.

"Well, we are getting married in jail, that's all there is to it," I answered. "They won't release him to marry in a church. I'm just hoping they let Celine be my maid of honor. Jack is guarded all the time in handcuffs. The best I can hope for is maybe the judge's chambers."

The celery stuffed with cream cheese went well with the white wine, and we were all hungry. We chatted a little about *Ecstasy* and Hedy Lamarr. John said her face was beautiful, but he found her body lacking. "After you and Jack get married, what then?" he asked. "Well, you know we plan to get a bigger apartment because of Joan's baby. But first I'll go back to Detroit with Jack and get a defense job for a while. Jack will probably get a ship again once he's freed on bail and can get it straightened out at the union hall."

John speculated that maybe the court wouldn't let him leave the state, which I had never thought of. But as of September 1st the apartment lease was up and we would have no place to live for a while. Immediately Celine said, "You can live in Pelham, there is plenty of room."

It was nice to hear, but I said, "Now that my sister is going to college in Washington, I'll have to go home to live with my mother. She gets lonesome without us and she has been supporting me all this time. When Jack is around, he comes first of course. But he won't want to live with my mom in Grosse Pointe, any more than I would want to live in Ozone Park with his parents. God! That would be the living end!"

By then it was starting to get very windy and cool. The horses on the bridle path were whinnying and that, I knew, was a sign of a weather change. We picked up everything and literally scampered off.

It was just getting dark when we got back to John's, and Celine and I put away the hamper and then went in to listen to some records. We were in the mood for Glenn Miller. We talked about Lucien's trial as we listened to the music. We speculated which of us would have to testify on the witness stand. It would be pretty funny if Allen began spouting about Dostoyevsky's "New Vision." We all admired the Russians; they were true bohemians. I said I wasn't looking forward to being called as a witness. I disliked Dave so I could hardly be unbiased. They both agreed that they felt the same way about him, Celine even more so. We sat silent, listening to Miller's "Sunrise Serenade," until it was time to go. John offered to walk us to the subway. We were both pretty tired by the time we pulled into Celine's house around midnight. Her brother had left a note that said, "Sis, I won't be back till morn. Cover for me. Thanks! P.S. Woof-it had dinner and long walk—I miss a dog around here. xxoo, Phil."

chapter 23

I awoke to the most delicious smell in the world: gingerbread cake and coffee. I got dressed and went downstairs and read the paper, but there was nothing in it. I brought a cup of coffee to the back yard and listened to the birds and thought of Jack. After a while I heard Celine in the kitchen. She came out and sat with me in the yard. Poor thing, she looked terrible. "Didn't you sleep well?" I asked.

"No, I tossed and turned and then had nightmares," she said. We always enjoyed delving into the details of our dreams. Burroughs had made us aware of our subconscious thoughts and we discussed them at length with each other. "It was Lucien, at the trial. He was found guilty. Then I had to witness his electrocution. I was strapped down, too, so I couldn't move. Then the reporters repeatedly raped me and Lucien had to watch as part of his sentence. I woke up before they pulled the switch on him."

"That's horrible. Bill would say you are suffering guilt feelings, you have to read something light and cheerful before you sleep. That's why I read Rose Franklyn. You know, something about happy married people in Connecticut with no problems. It's just the ticket for a troubled mind," I advised her. "Well, I wonder what our boys are doing this morning. Maybe they made them go to church."

"That's the only way you would get them there," Celine said sarcastically. Celine and I decided to make one last trip to the apartment to finish packing. Climbing the five flights of stairs for the last time to apartment 62 gave me a very nostalgic feeling. I opened the door and walked in, and noticed at once the odor of cat, dampness, and paint. I always painted there. We opened the windows and the breeze blew in and freshened the air while we set about packing the last of the clothes and books. A mattress and a red leather ottoman were the only things left in the living room. The bookcases were almost empty except for a few law books that belonged to Joan's husband, Paul. I decided to leave them behind since they'd be obsolete by the time Paul came back from the war. Celine picked up the broom and started to sweep the place. We only had throw rugs on the floor. Usually we would shake them out the window. I remembered one time when Jack shook the large round cotton rug out the window and he dropped it into the courtyard below. It took him hours to retrieve it, but he found ten dollars lying next to it, so he felt the effort had been worthwhile.

I snapped out of my daydreams and stacked the boxes near the front door for the movers. We called it quits and went to the tearoom in Gram's building for a delicious Sunday chicken dinner. While we were eating, Kingsland walked by and joined us. He said he had been looking for Ginsberg in the dorms but no one had seen him, so we figured he had gone home to New Jersey.

John wanted to come to the wedding. "I'm sorry, John, it would be impossible," I said. "I don't even know where it's going to take place. In the judge's chambers, the marriage bureau or somewhere else. Who knows? Jack is taking care of that. I'll find out Monday when I visit him." I charged the meal to my grandmother and we left.

By late afternoon we were back at Celine's house in Pelham. Strange, but that was the one place Jack had never been with me. He had visited every important place in my life but here. When we first fell in love, we wanted to feel, taste and touch everything that was important to each of us, the things that made us think and feel as we did. Because of our different backgrounds we had experienced life in very different ways. For instance, his Catholic upbringing was different from mine. I had gone to Sunday school and church but it did not have the mysticism of Jack's experiences or all the saintly folk stories it provided him. Jack wanted to hear about my stories of the super rich in Grosse Pointe, and about my family's farm in Dexter, and the Detroit Yacht Club and Asbury Park. Nothing in our lives was the same, yet here we were, about to get married tomorrow, or maybe the day after, but soon.

Finally Allen called. He said that John had told him that we were looking for him. "Is it anything important?" he asked.

"No, I just wanted to talk and see how you were doing," I told him.

"I tried to see Lucien," Allen said, "but they wouldn't let me.

They told me no visitors, only family. Well, I wish you luck on your marriage. You and Jack have been living together so long I guess it feels like a small thing to finally get hitched," he said. "I'm calling from Jersey, so I'll make it short. Best of luck to you both. I will see you soon, I hope. Tell Celine I am thinking of her. Farewell, and good-bye." He hung up.

Celine and I stayed up late that night, talking about the future and our most intimate thoughts and dreams. We agreed to visit each other in Paris when we lived there. I was sure Jack and I would get there. Wouldn't it be wonderful if we all ended up in an apartment there, like we had here? Only Joan was exempt from the burning desire to live in Europe. New York City was her Mecca and honestly, it was ours too.

chapter 24

. . .

Monday, August 21, 1944

I raced to get ready in the morning. I wanted to see Jack as early as I could and find out what he had arranged for our wedding. Then I had to call the lawyer and tell him so he could secure the bail money. "Yippee!" I thought, tomorrow will be my wedding day. I laughed to myself when I thought of my snobby Grosse Pointe pals and what they would think of my marrying a jailbird. Soon, when his books began to sell, we would have plenty of money and live in Connecticut some day, after Paris, of course. Then the children would come along. The only gloom I had was for our lost baby.

When you are young, you seem to be aware of only the good times, never the bad. As you grow older, you think first of what might go wrong and everything becomes negative. Only slowly, like sunshine coming through a cloudy sky, do you have flashes of good thoughts. Youth has few clouds; it's all sunshine. I looked to my marriage as the beginning to the end of all my problems, which were mostly tied to my family, money and security. One more day and Jack and I would be on our own. With our positive outlook on things I knew all would be fine, and I kept giving myself pep talks.

I was sorry my sister couldn't be with me, but it was out of the question. Gram was too wise to fool, so it was best not to say anything. This time the jail was packed with visitors. Jack came in with a lot of gruff looking prisoners. He looked lost as he tried to blend in with the rest of them. His still-tan skin revealed that he was not an old timer. He sat down and held my hand under the bars. I was surprised by his outward show of affection. "Everything okay with you, Jack?" I asked.

He said he had talked to Grumet who spoke to the judge and it looked as if we would be getting married the next day, Tuesday, August 22, 1944. "I'll know today for sure," he said. "Since they reduced the charge to material witness and the bond to $2,500, they must be anxious to get rid of me. So tomorrow, come dressed for our wedding. I can wear a sports jacket and tie, if you bring them. Say, where are my clothes?" he asked.

"Hanging in Gram's storage bin," I told him. "They're easy to get to, thanks to Jessie and Ward. I'll bring them. Now, what have you heard about Lucien?" I asked.

"Nothing really, he isn't here. They have him in the Tombs* downtown," he said.

"Poor Celine is a wreck. She's trying to get a full-time job as a

---

* The Tombs. Street slang for the New York City jail on Centre Street.

secretary for the winter. But with all the war brides around, there is a lot of competition, so she doesn't have much of a chance." Then Jack said, "We're broke, you know, so how do we live after I get out?"

"I think the thing to do is live with my folks. Woof-it, KitKat, you and I can live in my room for a while," I offered.

"I have to get the merchant marines straightened out. I think my ship, the *S.S. Robert Paine*, has left port," Jack said.

"I'll call your mother and see what she has to say. I'll tell her that we're getting married, but I'll say that the police will be the only ones there. Then they won't want to come. I won't tell her when or else they'll show up, under the guise that they didn't understand."

They rang a bell that indicated it was time to leave. "Well, I have a lot to do, so I'll go. Do you need any dimes? I have some," I said. I always carried a change purse for the telephone.

"Yeah, it would help," he said, so I dug into my bag which looked like a brown leather Pony Express pouch. They were all the rage then. We kissed through the bars before I left.

Back at Celine's I wrote letters to my mother, dad, Sis, and brother Bill. I sure wished someone in my family could be at my wedding, but it definitely wasn't going to happen. I could tell my brother and maybe my father, but how in hell could I explain the circumstances to them? It's something you can't do in a letter.

I had sent three of Jack's stories out to *Colliers*, *True Confessions* and *Esquire,* but for the time being we only had a total of $26. I would have to ask my mother for all our fares and try to explain that Jack had not committed any crime, despite the fact he was being treated like he had. For some reason, I had the terrible feeling that I would not be back in New York as a resident ever again. I definitely didn't like the feeling. When I finally came out of these dark thoughts, I found myself missing the apartment and Columbia, wishing I was there and not in Pelham.

Celine was lucky enough to find a part-time job and I told her about the plans Jack had made for the wedding. "Then we'll go to Grosse Pointe and recoup our finances," I said. "I'll get a defense job while Jack is at sea. My mother is alone now, so I should stay with her and help out on the farm driving the tractors. They'll be harvesting the alfalfa and hay in two weeks and they like me to help. It really is a bitch with no men to harvest or cut wood for the green houses in the winter. I wish you could see the farm Celine, it's huge and beautiful. Jack and I are crazy about it. We would love to stay there for a whole summer. That's the only thing he likes about Michigan, the farm in Dexter. Maybe you can visit me in the fall when your job is over. You know, a long time ago there was a settler's house right next to the road, built with the most gorgeous matched fieldstone. A fire demolished it and now there are vines covering the whole thing, but if you look closely the stones are still there. My grandfather said I could have them to use to build my own house someday." Celine reached over and patted my hand, "Things will work out, I know they will."

That evening after dinner was cleared, I told Celine I had to get the groom's outfit together. "Let's hope they let him change." Sleeping was hard for me in Pelham; it was too quiet, I had grown to love the big city's rumble and garbage can banging early in the mornings. The sound of the street vendors calling out their wares is muted six stories up. To live up high in a building in New York is wonderful. You have the warmth of the sun and a continuous concert of sirens, traffic horns, barking dogs, ringing telephones and whistling people.

It's a music that should be played in the desolate cities of gravestones you see when you drive through Queens and Brooklyn. It would make everything more natural for the dead.

Those were my thoughts as I fell asleep to little black cocker spaniel snores.

chapter 25

. . .

Tuesday, August 22, 1944. OUR WEDDING DAY

I woke up to Celine singing softly and Woof-it sitting patiently by my door, waiting to go outside. I opened the door and she raced for the kitchen. Then I heard Celine talking to her and the back door open, so I went back to sleep. After a few minutes, Woof-it was on the bed waking me up. Celine peeked in and said, "I'm running your bath. Me thinketh the bride should arise." I laughed and replied, "It is a golden morning, Maid Marion. I thank thee." Up and into the tub I went.

"I shall help mistress with her gown and hair," Celine said. "How about a cup of substance?" Celine returned with coffee and said, "All of Nottingham is waiting." Then I said, "Not to mention the inmates in the slammer." We laughed—it was a happy day.

Celine wore a plain dress buttoned down the front with the

two top and two bottom buttons open. Her shoes and purse matched her dress and she had blue combs to draw back her thick blond hair. She also wore white gloves, which were the fashion that summer. We both wore silver jewelry. She and I each had heavy chain identification bracelets. Hers was from Lucien, mine was from Jack, engraved with our names on the front and the boys' names on the back. "With Love," they said, and the dates. I.D. bracelets were the rage, I think it stemmed from army dog tags. We also wore silver ankle bracelets, too. Our names were engraved with those of the boys on back with the dates of our "anniversaries." These bracelets looked fabulous with a sun tan and all the girls wore them.

We stopped in the city, near Columbia, to pick up corsages. Mine, red roses (Jack's favorite) and Celine, sweet peas; both had bows of blue and white. I wore a blue garter belt I found in Gram's apartment so I was covered for something borrowed and something blue. We stopped for breakfast at the Chock Full O'Nuts near the Columbia gates, but I could hardly eat, I was so excited. Celine was cucumber cool. Well, I thought, why not be nervous, I'm the bride.

We opened up some windows in Gram's apartment to let the stuffiness out and I went down and got Jack's things from the basement. I grabbed his black-and-white plaid sports jacket, a white oxford shirt, his favorite red bow tie and dark pants. Also, a change of underthings and dark cotton socks. I asked Celine if we should get Jack a boutonniere, but we decided not to. Handcuffs and a boutonniere seemed absurd.

Before long it was time to go. By ten we were at the Bronx jail. Jack's clothes were sent up and Celine and I waited, first in the sergeant's room and then in the detective's office until after eleven, when they finally brought him down. Jack looked great, he was just beaming. I could tell he and the detective had had a few nips. They were both acting kind of silly leering at us; I felt like a canary.

"Is everyone set?" asked the detective. "Do you have the marriage license and your birth certificates?"

"Yes," I said, so we all piled into a cab down to the Municipal Building in lower Manhattan. Celine was sitting in the front seat and Jack was in the middle of the back seat between the detective and me. It was a hairy ride and we hung on to the straps for dear life without talking. The ride fit my jittery mood. I noticed they weren't using handcuffs on Jack and I was happy. We got to City Hall around 12:30 and I thought, "I bet they're closed."

We all walked up the worn granite stairs, turned to the right, and got on the elevator to the second floor. Jack and I then stepped up to a brass cage where the City Clerk, W. Warren Huffault, asked for our marriage license, birth certificates and the twenty dollar fee. Jack only had his baptismal certificate which stated that he had made his first communion on May 17, 1928 and had been baptized on March 12, 1922, seven days after his birth. The clerk pointed out that our license had expired. "What do you mean, expired?" I shouted. He told me the license was good for only twenty-four hours and it was now twelve hours past that time. To my embarrassment, Detective John flashed his badge to the clerk and said, "This man is my prisoner and we only have a certain amount of time until he has to get back. What do you suggest I do?" The clerk told us to go up to the judge's chambers anyway, because the war was causing them to loosen their rules a bit.

On the way to see the judge, I was aware that everyone was looking at us, me in particular. Naturally, they must have thought I was pregnant. We schlepped up to the third floor where all the courtrooms and judges were located. Only one door was open and it appeared as if a trial was wrapping up just as we arrived, all very intimidating under the circumstances.

Detective John went in to talk to another clerk, but first he handcuffed Jack to his wrist. He reminded him, "These are judges and you are my prisoner." Detective John and Jack were taken to the chambers of Judge Manninger Shawl while Celine and I sat and waited on a wooden pew in the back of the courtroom. The judge sent his clerk out to do the necessary paperwork and we waited almost half an hour without knowing what was going on.

Finally the clerk returned and went into the judge's chambers. As Celine and I waited, I noticed the heavy bars on all the windows. Since we were on the third floor, I wondered who would try to escape from this place? At last they called us into the judge's chambers where Celine and I were introduced to the judge. Judge Shawl was a small muscular man with a large head of graying curly hair and a Van Dyke beard. He remained seated throughout the introductions, which I found very rude. "I will perform the ceremony right now," he stated bluntly. "Will you please stand over there?"

When he finally stood up, he was so short that you could hardly notice he had risen at all. Celine and I could barely keep from snickering, but we did. Judge Shawl then asked Detective McKeon to keep his prisoner confined during the ceremony. "What an ass!" I thought.

Just then his clerk interrupted and the judge left to tend to something out in the courtroom. It seemed to take forever, but once he returned he asked us all to, "Please rise." He placed Celine to my left and Jack to my right, with Jack still hand-cuffed to McKeon. "I shall begin," he said.

I slipped our silver friendship rings into the judge's pocket, the ones Jack and I had purchased at Tiffany's. We had both been wearing them on the engagement fingers of our left hands for more than a year. Jack bought them for fifty dollars apiece after his voyage to England during the war. There was a hefty twenty percent tax on all jewelry, if you could even find it to buy, since silver and gold were needed for the war effort.

Judge Shawl called in his clerk, Murray Stand, and began to recite the vows. "Will you take this woman for better or for worse, in sickness and in health?" He did not ask, "Who gives this woman in holy matrimony?" But continued, "Then under the eyes of God and this court, I pronounce you man and wife. You may kiss the bride." Jack did, the judge disappeared back behind his desk and Murray offered his congratulations as he escorted us out to the corridor. Then he handed me a marriage certificate with the seal of New York and the time, 1:48 P.M. and the date, August 22, 1944. The actual marriage was performed at 2:57 P.M. with Detective John McKeon as the only signed witness. They never even asked Celine to sign as a witness.

As we were going downstairs on a huge, old, rickety eleva-tor, John took the cuffs off Jack and said he needed a drink. Jack and I were relieved since we had wondered what would happen after the ceremony. A drink sounded like a good idea. John knew of an old pub near the post office, just a block away. The pub turned out to be a little farther away than John

Jack and Edie's marriage certificate, 1944.

recalled, but before long we arrived and found a large semi-round booth. They ordered champagne for Celine and me and boiler makers (beer and whiskey) for them. I could tell that

Jack was trying to impress McKeon by posing as a hard-drinking merchant seaman.

After a few toasts to the bride and groom, John said to Jack, "Remember, I have a gun if you're thinkin' about any funny stuff." He said it with a half-smile, but it put a damper on our celebration. Jack raised his glass to me and said, "Here's looking at you kid" with his best Bogart sneer and lisp. John laughed at that and said, "You been living together, so it ain't like you was a virgin." He spoiled the whole romantic mood with his crude remark, and I remember thinking that you could tell he was a cop. Celine broke the tension by suggesting we go powder our noses. In the ladies room, Celine told me not to let McKeon spoil my wedding day. I agreed and went to the pay phone to call Kennedy, our lawyer. I told him we were married and he should start the wheels rolling to get the emergency loan. He asked where we were as he had to come to pick up the proof of our marriage.

When Kennedy arrived a short time later, I introduced him around. He congratulated Jack, telling him that he'd known me since I was a little girl and warned him to take good care of me. Jack looked miserably embarrassed as he muttered, "I'll try, sir." With that, I took Herbert by the arm to sit at another table, out of earshot of the others. I handed him the license and he had me sign some papers. I gave him the address of Jack's parents in Ozone Park, Queens, and he said he would make copies and send them there. Before he left he wished Jack good luck and told him he had married a fine girl from a good family of good stock. I said that his comment made me feel like a horse being auctioned off, and we all laughed about it.

Jack suggested that we all go to O'Henry's for a steak.

"What do you say, McKeon?" he asked. It seemed fine with the detective, and Jack knew it was one of my favorite places. John paid the tab at the bar and we all hopped into a cab and headed down to O'Henry's. A converted butcher shop, O'Henry's was a very unusual type of restaurant. There were meat hooks hanging from the tin ceiling and sawdust spread over the white tile floor. Customers selected their own steaks from a meat case and they tagged it with well, medium or rare and your last name. The young boys who worked there wore James Cagney Yankee Doodle Dandy straw hats with red, white and blue ribbons. They used arm bands to hold up their long white shirt sleeves and wore buttons that said "Vote for O'Henry." It was all topped off by fake handlebar mustaches. Each table had red-and-white checkered tablecloths and blue dishware. All the waiters wore white butcher's aprons from waist to ankle and sang barbershop songs from the 1800s as they served.

We got there at 4:30 and were seated just before people started to line up. To have any meat at all near the end of the war was a rare treat. It was a sort of western, family-style place, and once seated everyone became friends and carried on crazy conversations. The menus were written on blackboards and hung on the walls. Each table was given a soup tureen filled with fresh-baked kosher rolls and crocks of butter. It really had such a wonderful feel about it that you would find yourself humming and singing along with the waiters. Whenever anyone hit a long, loud high note, one of the waiters would blow a whistle. We ordered pitchers of beer with frozen stone mugs emblazoned with O'Henry's logo.

Being just married, with my love almost out of jail and the

beer and the food, I was in heaven! Everyone was singing and we joined in. When our steaks came it was pure joy to cut into them, and we never spoke until we were done. All the people who weren't eating were singing. New York back then was a singing town. Notice that I didn't say happy town, for people sang to hide their sadness and keep their spirits up.

We finished our fabulous meal, but before we had coffee and dessert, a clown came by with a money box asking what we'd had to eat and we paid him at the table. Celine, a born flirt, had gotten pretty chummy with McKeon and he paid for her meal. He didn't realize that was the whole point of her flirtation, but Jack and I knew and kept giving each other knowing winks. It always worried us when she would carry these flirtations too far in the bedroom and then barely manage to slip out. She did this a lot in our apartment. The sailors she would bring around never took this very well and would sometimes pound on the door to our room, madder than hell. Sometimes Jack would patiently get up and make coffee for the poor slob and talk with him, and eventually he would leave. Celine was always doing this, but Lucien was the only one she slept with, and even that was after months of courting. Jack and I called her a professional virgin.

Jack paid for our dinner that night at O'Henry's, after I slipped him the money under the table. We all had coffee, and Celine and I had wonderful lemon meringue pie five inches high. Jack and John capped it off with brandy and cigars. The clown came back with our change and we left. It was about seven, and McKeon had to get Jack back to the jail. We lingered outside waiting for a cab. Jack and I embraced while Celine and McKeon necked up a storm. When the cab arrived,

McKeon slipped Celine his card and told her to call him at that number at nine o'clock. Jack and I were quiet but spoke to each other with our eyes. It was very sad. As he got into the cab Jack looked back at me and said, "I'll be thinking of us tonight and all the nights to come." I was too choked up to answer him. The cab started to pull away and I could see McKeon putting the cuffs back on Jack's wrists. I started to sob and Celine put her arm around me as we walked slowly to the subway station.

We had decided to go to Celine's mother's house in Pelham, where we arrived about nine. Celine's mother was having tea and a piece of cake in the kitchen while I sat down in their living room imagining the day when Jack and I would have a house like that one. Just then the phone rang and Celine jumped up to answer it. She told her mother it was an answering service wanting her to be interviewed for a job first thing in the morning. Celine went upstairs to bed and I followed right behind her, knowing this was a phony excuse to get out of the house. I asked what was up and she said, "That was McKeon on the phone. Once mom's asleep I'll take a cab and meet him at the Roosevelt Hotel. He said he can get me a pass to see Lucien. It's the only chance I have." I told her that it was a hell of a price to pay, but she assured me it wasn't that bad. I shrugged my shoulders and went into my room, but could hardly sleep. You can imagine the turmoil in my head that night. I read Dos Passos for hours and eventually fell asleep.

STUDENT IS INDICTED IN 2D-DEGREE MURDER

Lucien Carr, 19-year-old Columbia University sophomore, was indicted yesterday for second-degree murder in the stabbing of David Kammerer, 33, on Aug. 14. At the same time the police revealed that they had uncovered a second material witness, William Seward Borroughs, 30, of 69 Bedford Street. He is free in bail of $2,500, set by General Sessions Judge John J. Sullivan, before whom young Carr will plead to the indictment Tuesday.

Borroughs, the police said, admitted that after Carr had stabbed Kammerer, former college instructor, and then weighted his body with rocks and tossed it into the Hudson River, he had heard the story from the youth and had done nothing because Carr said he was on his way to surrender. It was almost twenty-four hours later before Carr gave himself up.

After Carr had told Borroughs he repeated the story to John Kerouac, former Columbia student, who has been held as a materail witness in default of $5,000 bail. The police escorted Kerouac to the Municipal Building on Tuesday to witness his marriage to Miss Edith Parker of Detroit and then took him back to Bronx prison.

chapter 26

It was nearly ten in the morning when I woke to an empty
house. I was planning to see Jack that afternoon and hoped he
wouldn't be worried about me. Jack had been in the slammer
for a week. I showered and dressed, wishing I was at the
seashore and could go for a morning swim. As I ate my breakfast the phone rang. It was Gabe Kerouac saying her "Jackie"
had called that morning to tell her the good news. She was
tickled pink, one of her favorite expressions, because Jack and I
would be coming to live with them after Jack got out of jail.
After I hung up, I thought that it might not be too bad to live
with Jack's mother, but his father, well, that was another matter
entirely. He stopped me cold from even wanting to consider it.

Then I called my lawyer to find out what was going on with
the probate judge back in Detroit. He said the matter would
be taken up that day and that I should call back at three that

afternoon. Since I had a few minutes I decided to take Woof-it to the park before the summer heat got too bad. Sitting by the park fountain I felt apprehensive about our future. Jack would have to ship out soon to earn some money and I would be wanting a home and family. The idea of working in a factory or some such thing did not appeal to me anymore. The work never bothered me; earning enough to fix up a home and make it pretty for Jack excited me as I sat there daydreaming.

That day, August 23, I went to visit my husband, Jack, around one in the afternoon. He was wearing a white short sleeve dress shirt and chino pants. Since I hoped he was getting out that day, I didn't want to lay my concerns on him. We only had to wait for word that the judge in Detroit had granted my petition and had released my trust money so that I could post Jack's bail. When Jack asked me what was going on, I had to admit that I was still in the dark. He was getting nervous but I assured him that I was going to Kennedy's office directly and that he would soon be out and everything would be okay. I told him about his mother's call and that she wanted us out in Ozone Park as soon as possible, and I said I would go, even if I would feel very uncomfortable there. "Do what you want, but first get me out of here," he said. We held hands, our wedding rings touching. The police gave me greater access now because we were married, so we could touch and even kiss through the bars.

I timed it to get to Herbert Kennedy's office at three, but before going in to see him I grabbed a hotdog from a cart near the Fulton Fish Market and downed it as fast as I could. When I arrived Kennedy was not back from court yet, so I sat and waited, flipping through old *Look* and *Life* magazines. After a short while Herbert came in and looked surprised to see me.

There was something about him I never did like. He seemed nice, but also a little slick. He brought me into his office and gestured for me to have a seat. Judge O'Donnell had given his permission to release $500 from the trust fund for Jack's bond, conditional on the money being returned after Jack had appeared as a witness at Lucien's trial, all of which was fine with me. Herbert told me they would be arraigning Jack the next morning and he would do what he could to have the charges against Jack reduced and have his bail lowered. I signed five papers, all in triplicate, and then Herbert handed me a $500 check and told me to go to the bail bond office downtown in the same place where I had gotten our marriage license. They would give me a paper to take to the Bronx County jail and Jack would be released.

I walked, almost ran, to the bail bond office where I arrived just as they were about to close. Fortunately they had been notified by the County Clerk and were expecting me, so they let me in. I gave them the check and they handed me Jack's release form, signed, sealed and delivered. I couldn't believe everything went off without a hitch. I glanced up at the clock, hoping I could get to the jail in time to get Jack released, and then headed for the uptown B.M.T subway to the Grand Concourse in the Bronx. I got to the police station and stated my business to the desk sergeant, showing him the release document. He looked at it, smiled, then called for Detective O'Donnell to come down. O'Donnell arrived and was very friendly, "How's your friend, Celine?" he asked. "Fine," I said, wondering where she was myself. While I waited for Jack I called her house to find out if it was okay for Jack to come to Pelham with me. Her mother answered and told me Celine was out somewhere, but said it would be fine for me to bring Jack. "That's wonderful! We'll have a little party. Ask John Kingsland and whomever you wish," she said. But I knew no one would come, they'd all gone underground.

I hung up and waited for them to bring Jack down. In thirty minutes my husband would be with me—minus the handcuffs. I had to pinch myself. The past nine days had truly felt like nine years. Suddenly, there he was standing before me, I could hardly believe it. We said goodbye to the cops as we left, but they were snickering, making crude wise-ass remarks. Finally we were alone out on the street, hugging and kissing and shaking with happiness. We went straight to the Oyster Bar for a much-needed drink. Jack had a whiskey on the rocks, I stuck with a soft drink, and for the first time through all of the ordeal we were finally able to relax. Jack held my hand and told me how glad he was to get out and thanked me for coming up with the money.

Jack always tried to be humble. He would say that if there was one goal he hoped to achieve in his lifetime, that was it. "Well, what's on the ticket next?" he asked.

"We're going to catch the train up to Celine's for a small party and spend the night there. Then I'm hoping tomorrow Kingsland will drive us and the animals and our bags to your parents' house," I answered. Jack said he had a gas ration book he could give to John for the trip. I handed him ten dollars for our tab and the train fare. He said he had some money stashed at Gabe's and would give me back my ten dollars when we got there. "Why? What's yours is mine and vice versa," I said, but I noticed he never answered.

Jack stopped to buy all the newspapers, and during the ride

was deeply engrossed in them. "What bank does your mother use?" I asked, just to make conversation. "She keeps it in the cookie jar," he mumbled, "actually in an old blue tea pot. Leo has a savings account somewhere in Lowell, I think." Then I asked if he was kidding, but he said he wasn't and went back to reading his paper. "Your family is really different from mine," I said.

Reluctantly, Jack put the paper aside and said, "My parents lost all their money when their bank went under during the Depression, and Mémère said she would never put any money in a bank again. I tried to explain to her that it was different now, but she won't hear it. She isn't a business woman like your mother."

He went back to his paper and I took out my book—Saroyan, I loved him. Jack did, too. We saw the movie, *Human Comedy*, several times even though Jack said, "There's no mention of the story."

We arrived at the Pelham station a little after six, where we were greeted by Celine and Kingsland and Woof-it, who sported a white bow with silver bells. Jack grinned from ear to ear. As we got into the car they both started humming "Here Comes The Bride" and threw confetti at us. Then we all drove off to Celine's for a celebration feast. On the way, she told me that Joan planned to call later.

Celine's mother and her neighbor Celeste greeted us at their door and threw more confetti. As we entered the house they handed each of us a glass of champagne and shouted, "Kiss the bride!" embarrassing Jack. We gathered in the dining room where our meal was all laid out and waiting. There was a huge bouquet of lilies, daisies, and stephanotis with a large white ribbon to match the flowers. Joan had sent them, it was so lovely. Jack and I sat at one end of the table, Celine and John at the other. We dove into the food while Celine and John clanked their forks on the glasses so we would kiss, so nice and provincial and corny. Celine said she had asked Jack's family to come, but unfortunately they both had to work and missed the celebration. Gabe asked Celine to tell us she would have a surprise of her own for us when we arrived the next night. Jack wasn't all that sorry they weren't there, painfully embarrassing as it all was to him. He was drinking wine, a lot of wine, but he sure could use it since he had really been through the mill.

We listened to WEXL on the radio, and the announcer unexpectedly broke in to congratulate us on our marriage. At first Jack was stunned, then angry. "Who did that anyway, huh?" he demanded. No one answered. He seemed to get over it quickly, but he reminded me of his father when he spoke angrily like that.

He sat gloomily in silence at the table for a while until Celine and her mother brought in the wedding cake. It was decorated with phony flowers and a bride and groom on top. "This is from our friends at the bakery. The bride and groom are from my wedding cake," Mrs. Young said proudly. Everyone felt a little sad because Mr. Young was gone. The cake was angel food with thick gooey icing. We all went at it with gusto and by the time we finished there was little left and Jack was finally able to relax.

By 9:00 it was all over. Kingsland fell asleep on the sofa, intending to drive us to Ozone Park the next day. I suggested to Jack that we take Woof-it out for a walk to my favorite spot in the park. We changed into casual clothes and headed out into the cool night air, away from the cigarette smoke and candles. We walked into the park through the wrought iron gate to the fountain I loved so much. I said to Jack, "It isn't the Trevi in Rome, just Pelham's answer to it." It seemed that since Jack had been released from jail, my jokes were no longer funny to him and he didn't even chuckle. Everybody else always laughed at my jokes, but Jack had a serious way about him. He looked at life as a bad tasting medicine, whereas I saw it all through rose colored glasses. It seemed that Henri Cru's sense of humor fit mine much better than Jack's did. Jack's humor escaped me. He thought people's antics were funny, and he didn't appreciate more cerebral humor like that of W.C. Fields or Groucho Marx. Instead he preferred the Three Stooges, they were funny to him.

We sat down on the bench beside the fountain and let Woof-it run around off his leash. "Well, we've done it, haven't we?" Jack declared. "Done it?" I wondered. "You mean getting married? I thought we were practically married when we started living together."

"No, no. You know what I mean. It's serious, us together forever," he continued.

"You always see everything as being our last breath on earth. Lighten up, will you?" I said. "Yes, we're married. You heard the judge; through sickness and health. For rich or poor. Let's enjoy the park and this evening. You're out of jail and everything will be okay."

"Yeah, you're right, but how am I going to pay back that $500 to your mother?" he worried.

I began to recite Poe's "Annabel Lee." "It was many and many a year ago/ In a kingdom by the sea/ That a maiden there lived whom you may know/ By the name of Annabel Lee." I never could remember it all the way through, but Jack didn't mind, he enjoyed correcting me. It distracted him and put him in a better frame of mind. "You'll sure have plenty to write about. This past month has equaled an entire lifetime of experiences. There are few writers who have spent time in the slammer!" I laughed, but Jack could not see the humor in any of it.

"Let's go back to the house, I'm anxious to get you to bed," Jack suggested. I looked at him surprised, this was out of character for him. It was about 10:30 when we got back. Everyone was in bed and John was out cold on the sofa. The house was completely still. We crept upstairs quietly to our room for the first night of our honeymoon. I can remember we both trembled when our bare skin touched. Then Jack's masculine strength took over. He had the most delicious scent about him, I was always excited by it. We clung to each other for that glorious moment and knew we belonged together. We made love, and only when we finally came back down to earth did I hope we hadn't made too much noise. I can't say I really knew. Jack fell asleep on his back, his right arm extended above his head as he always did. I snuggled close and slept soundly, feeling complete at last.

chapter 27

. . .

The next morning I awoke and was surprised to see Jack in the same position as when he'd fallen asleep. He must have really been exhausted from his ordeal. I got up silently and went to the bathroom to put on a nighty before I crept back into bed, careful not to wake Woof-it or Jack. I slid back next to Jack's warmth, reassured to be lying next to my love while he slept, listening to his heart and breath. I almost stopped my own to listen closely to his. We were in unison and I wasn't conscious of my own heartbeat.

I was nudged out of my dreams by Woof-it, who had already woken Jack, too. Jack was deep in thought, almost meditative. As I got up and dressed, Jack reached for a Lucky Strike, nearly falling out of bed in the process. I said I would take Woof-it out while he showered, since I knew Kingsland would want to get going before long. Then, sounding too much like a wife, I told Jack not to read in the bathroom. He grunted and reached for the book on the night stand that he had been reading.

Downstairs John was already up and folding his bedding. "Good morning! Did you have a satisfying night?" he asked. "Yes, we did, thank you," I said coldly to put an abrupt end to his inquiry. I told him to make some coffee while I took Woof-it out for a quick stroll around the block. When I got back to the house Jack and John were talking about Jack's gas ration stamps. Jack had gotten them once as part of his pay, thinking Leo could use them. Most people living in Manhattan had no need for a car since public transportation was available. The war made the use of a car a luxury, especially because of rationing, and Jack really treasured those stamps since he felt they made him part of the driving population, even though he had no driver's license.

We said goodbye to Pelham and Celine's mother. Celine, we planned to see later back in the city. Then we all crammed into John's big Buick with the animals and me in the back seat. KitKat was in her traveling box on top of a pile of books and the trunk was filled with luggage. It took us the better part of an hour to drive to Ozone Park in Queens. As we got close to Jack's parents house he suggested we stop at a great diner he knew near Belmont Racetrack. He and his father went there, so he knew it was good. The diner was all shiny aluminum and squeaky clean. We each ordered corned beef hash with poached eggs on top and crispy home fries. We must have used half a bottle of catsup and drank a gallon of coffee, while we talked about communism and all that was going on in the world. John was staunchly against communism, but Jack was in favor of it for the depressed countries, even if he didn't think it was right for America. Remember, Russia was our ally during the war and communists were being killed by the thousands in Nazi-held territories. Many of our men were in the Pacific fighting the Japs at the time. If Russia hadn't sided with the Allies, I'm sure the outcome of the war would have been different. Jack was personally in touch with the fighting, whereas John was not. The discussion continued, even back in the car.

I can recall driving beneath the elevated subway tracks along Crossbay Boulevard where there was a lot of noise, but not many people. You couldn't even hear yourself talk when a train passed overhead. KitKat was so scared that Jack reached over to put his hand in her box to pet her, but in her fear she scratched him. He thought nothing of it, though, as he had a high tolerance for pain, due to his football experiences. I was the one always complaining about a toothache or some such pain, and Jack was always very compassionate and babied me. He would rub me with Vicks when I had a cold, or heat up a can of Campbell's tomato soup. It was his favorite, and he gave me cans of it on our honeymoon.

As we got closer to the Kerouac home at 133-01 Crossbay Boulevard, we passed fewer and fewer houses. Everything was sand and dunes. In the distance you could see tufts of tall salt grass here and there, waving a warm welcome to us as we approached the drugstore Jack's parents lived above. There were two apartments in the building. The other was occupied by a very sweet Jewish couple whose son was the famous actor, John Garfield. Garfield came for visits to look after his parents when they grew old. He and Jack became friends and took long walks on the sand dunes. They discussed the plots of Jack's short stories. They shared an interest in people. If Garfield hadn't become a big star, I think he too would have become a merchant seaman and writer, like Jack.

That day Jack bounded up the long stairway to the apartment, leaving me in the car. The stairs were on the outside of the building and lead up to a small, railed landing and the rear entrance to the house. I sat for a while in the car looking across the quiet boulevard to the vast emptiness and took in the entire scene.

After a few minutes I climbed out of the backseat with Woof-it. Since I was coming down with a cold, I hoped we would be going to bed soon. Jack had taken the cat up with him and when John and I walked in we saw Gabe treating Jack's scratches at the kitchen table. The kitchen was the largest room in the flat and the first room you entered as you walked in from the back. The bathroom was right off the kitchen. There was also a dining room and a living room. Jack's bedroom, where we would sleep for the next few weeks, was just off the living room. The front door opened to a varnished wood landing and stairway that led down to the drugstore.

Gabe had a custom of serving two main courses at "special" meals. She made us a wedding feast of ham and chicken with mashed potatoes, gravy, rutabaga and coleslaw. The dinner was delicious and so was the bottle of red wine Gabe brought out to celebrate. Leo was already a little tipsy by the time we arrived. His face was red and his bulbous nose glowed. That night he was on his very best behavior. In fact, it was the only meal I can remember when he didn't pick a fight with Jack. He also expected women to keep quiet when he was speaking and never offer an opinion. That was where Jack was very different, he was considerate. If Woof-it could have expressed herself, he would have listened.

Gabe bought fresh daisies for the table, which were a great luxury and expense. She didn't even like flowers but she wanted to makes things nice for us. For dessert she had prepared Jack's favorite, vanilla ice cream from the drugstore with fresh-baked chocolate brownies she'd made herself. She had been hoarding the ingredients for a long time. My mother thought very badly of people who hoarded during the war, and so did the government. There were signs in all the grocery stores asking people to do their part by not hoarding, and sugar in particular was a highly valued commodity.

Gabe and Leo both spoke with French accents and had a way of speaking English words in the wrong order which I thought was cute, but Jack was always attempting to correct them. They were both short—Leo was 5'2" and Gabe was about 5'0" and roly-poly. Leo always wore a black suit and white shirt, with his sleeves held up by old-fashioned gambler's arm bands. He was unkempt-looking, with wrinkled shirt, tie loosened and continually perspiring. He kept a handkerchief in his pocket which was always wet. I don't think Gabe neglected him once, ever. She was constantly washing and ironing, and her house was immaculate. Gabe was like a little doll who wore a clean house dress every day with a matching apron. In fact, I never saw her without an apron. Only when they had company or when she went to church did she remove it. She was always busy and happily hummed as she did the chores around the house. She was meant to be the caretaker of her family and this is what she wanted. I may have had that inclination once a week, but it didn't last long. Jack's mother was very feminine in her own way and also had a great curiosity, in fact she was forever asking me questions. She even looked in my closet and dresser drawers to see how I did things. She hoped to have a mirror image of herself to take care of her son. I accepted the challenge while I was there and tried to emulate everything she did, as she did it. I even wore my long hair in a bun like hers. Jack was pleased because his mother was pleased. He never noticed that I was only playing a role.

Gabe and Leo hadn't been living in New York very long, so they were still discovering the city, which was very different from the serious nuts and bolts, brass-tacks, blue collar town of Lowell. In New York they were like two kids who walked into a candy store with sacks of cash. Gabe planned our days and nights, while Jack and I just tried to get used to the idea of living with them.

chapter 28

. . .

Leo wanted us to go with him to the racetrack on our first full day there, so he woke us early that next morning. I got to the bathroom first, dressed and took Woof-it for a walk. It was a windy day, but especially windy in Ozone Park. The ocean was not far away and there was nothing to break the wind. While I was out, I waved at Gabe, who was standing on the corner waiting for her bus to work. Inside, Leo was scurrying around in the kitchen trying to make an omelet. I sat down at the table and had coffee while Leo ate his breakfast and Jack emerged from the bathroom with a book of Shakespeare's sonnets. Jack dove right in to Leo's egg creation and I was surprised to see how much he liked it. I guess it's all about what you're used to. While I straightened up the bathroom and made the beds, Jack and Leo tackled the kitchen cleanup so we could get going to Belmont Racetrack, a short walk from their apartment.

There we went directly to the stables where the grooms were rubbing down the horses after their morning workout. Everyone was busy brushing, feeding and walking those beautiful animals. Leo knew all the stable hands and the few jockeys that were around. The place was also loaded with dogs, at least one, if not two, to every stall. They were all sweet, calm mutts and they paid no attention to us as we petted the horses. I wanted to feed the horses some carrots or apples, but Jack told me that their diets were watched very closely. I was surprised by his knowledge of the ins and outs of the thoroughbred stables. He told me that when he was fourteen, he had been a stable boy in Nashua, NH, during his visit to his mother's brother, Uncle Joe.

"Do you see the extra riding horse with the grooms? Well, they and the dogs act as companions to the thoroughbreds to keep them calm. They're very jumpy and are prone to injuring themselves," Jack explained. Then he asked, "Would you like to see the starting gate?" We walked over to the track and Jack showed me how it worked, pulling the switches that opened and closed the gates. The field crew was preparing the dirt track for that afternoon's race by lightly turning it over with tractors.

When we got back, Leo was in the tack room drinking coffee laced with rum and discussing the horses and who would ride them that day. The jockeys were being assigned their horses and were picking up their colors to wear. Once dressed they weighed in before each race. Jack was writing down names in his little notebook. "Are we coming back to see them race?" I asked.

"If you want to, but I'm not going to bet, you know," he answered.

"I know, but it would still be great to see," I said. "I like the looks of Joan's Delite" and Jack agreed. "That's a good little filly, she has a great sire and a winning dam," he said. Then he proceeded to tell me all the horse's names and their stables. As he was talking, all I could think about was his incredible mind and memory. Leo was walking around puffing his cigar, acting as if he owned a race horse.

Before we lived with them, I thought I liked Leo. Despite his pompous personality he was funny in his own way, but he just didn't realize he was funny. We stayed at the track until lunchtime and then we walked back to the apartment. Leo left to make some business calls and Jack and I had lunch. "I'm tired so let's take a nap," Jack suggested. What he was really saying was that he wanted to make love, but he would never come right out and say it. For some reason that always excited me, and I couldn't wait.

By the time Gabe got home from work around five, Jack and I were up, refreshed, and well rested. Jack was sitting in the living room reading. When she came in, Gabe went over and gave him a kiss which Jack shrugged off. "Can't I kiss you now that you're married?" she asked. She chuckled and tousled his hair. Jack scowled and ran his fingers through it to straighten it. His pride was his thick head of curly black hair, which had been the second thing I noticed when we first met. The first, of course, was his beautiful blue eyes. I always got butterflies when I thought of our first meeting. I wondered what might have happened if I had stayed in Grosse Pointe; we would never have met.

I put some coffee on for all of us and brought out the rest of Gabe's brownies. She was so pleased and thanked me for keeping the place neat. Otherwise she'd have to do it after working her eight-hour shift at the factory. I knew exactly how she felt. After working all day as a longshoreman in the Brooklyn Navy Yard, I'd have to go home and clean up after everyone at our apartment. Leo came in and we all sat around the kitchen table sipping coffee and talking. Two years later Leo would die at that same table in his favorite chair, made of maple with seat and back cushions covered with an old scratchy plaid wool blanket.

Gabe suggested that we all go to Radio City Music Hall to see the Rockettes that night, "We haven't seen them this month. We haven't seen a movie either." Back then it was customary for the Rockettes to change their routine and costumes frequently. New Yorkers made it a point to see them once a month, a tradition. Jack asked me what I'd like to do, and I said it sounded like a great idea. Gabe and I made dinner and after that we were off to the city. When we arrived at Radio City we didn't have to stand in line very long. First they ran the Pathe News and then a Disney short before the feature film about pirates starring Gene Kelly. Next came an organ concert followed by the Rockettes, dressed in red, white and blue top hats and canes. They tap danced to patriotic songs from the First World War. They were terrific, and that evening there was even a surprise guest, Deanna Durbin, who sang a few songs leading up to a war bond pitch. It was nearly 11 P.M. by the time we left.

The four of us strolled over to Times Square. Leo had Gabe's hand and Jack held mine as we wended our way through the crowds of sailors, American, Russian, and British, all looking for that elusive woman. Gabe suggested we duck into the Brass Rail, one of her favorite places. The bar was half empty, which Leo said was because it was a "rip-off joint," since they had a five dollar minimum. Gabe loved sausage and sauerkraut, so we all ordered that with big steins of ice cold beer. We ate at the bar and while we were waiting for the food, Leo asked me to dance. He was a great dancer, one who walked you all around the dance floor. With a few shots of booze under his belt, he held me close to his perspiring body. I danced as brief a time as was politely possible. Jack didn't like to dance; he felt there was no point to it. I felt he was so gorgeous that he didn't have to bother with the small things, since every woman was attracted to him.

It seemed ironic that all these servicemen ate German cuisine. "We'll have to make an early night of it, I have to work, you know," Gabe said. It took an hour and a half to get home because we had to take a bus and the subway and only three buses an hour ran after midnight due to the gas shortage. You never saw much graffiti back then. The only thing you saw were posters on the trains like, "Kilroy Was Here" or "Buy Bonds for Bombs." The wooden boxes full of ammunition I loaded onto the ships at my job driving a hi-lo were all clearly stamped, "Inspected by R.V. Kilroy." That's where the slogan came from. We got home around 1:30 A.M. Jack walked Woof-it and afterwards we both fell asleep, very grateful to be together.

chapter 29
. . .

Jack liked to make love in the morning, so it was nearly ten
before we finally got up. The apartment was empty and Gabe
had left some coffee for us. Jack went to the bathroom to read
the Bible. He did that in the morning and read Shakespeare
in there at night. At breakfast Jack said, "We have to make our
plans to go to Michigan as soon as possible. I'm anxious to find
work to pay back the $500. And we're going to have to borrow
another $100 from your mother to get there. I'm going to write
her a letter today to ask her for the loan." Jack said Gabe had
left him a note saying Nin was coming up from Washington
on a 48-hour leave. She was recruiting secretaries for the
W.A.C.S., so I asked if there was anything I could do to help
Gabe prepare. Jack said Gabe would plan everything and the
best thing to do was to stay out of her way. I must have looked
hurt because Jack got up from the table, gave me a kiss and

told me, "That's how my parents are. They'll have every minute planned."

Then he walked into the bedroom and sat down at the table he used for a desk, bare but for an old goose-neck lamp and his typewriter. He began pounding away on his large Royal typewriter, faster than anyone I'd ever seen. In our apartment he had used a small Underwood that had a black leather case with a Columbia University emblem on it. He composed his letter to my mother, but it all sounded too businesslike. "You can't send this! It's too impersonal," I said. "After all, we're married now and don't have to hide anymore. Be a little kinder." I could feel his mood change and he rewrote it, softening it up a bit, and I added a little postscript of my own.

With his letter finished, Jack suggested we go to the union hall and see what was happening there. "As far as they know I'm still in jail," he said. "I'll have to face the music sooner or later. We can see about your joining like you mentioned. With your Red Cross ambulance certificate and belonging to the longshoreman's union I can't see how you could miss." So we went to the union hall where all the seamen gathered to pick up their pay and get new jobs on the ships. It was a fascinating place. On a huge blackboard were the names of various ships, their companies, captains, cargos, ship-out dates, pier locations and whatever classification was needed, Able Bodied, Electrician, Mates, First or Second Class. As the positions were filled they were erased by a man on a ladder. It reminded me of the stock exchange, except the seamen didn't wear business suits, instead they wore cast off navy garb purchased at the Salvation Army or P.X. (if they had a pass to get in).

Jack was always looking for "Big Slim" Hazzard, a man who

had been in the navy psych ward with him. Big Slim was from New Orleans and usually shipped out from there, but he would occasionally dock in New York. Jack asked everyone he knew if they had seen Big Slim or "Old Religious Glory," the cook from the *S.S. Weems*. The last time he had seen him, Jack said, they had a "rip snorting" good time. The purser asked Jack if he'd be interested in catching a ship carrying live ammo to the Pacific. "Lots of bonuses," he said. The waters were full of German mines and subs that sat waiting off the coast, so Jack passed on those ships. Once, Henri Cru had been torpedoed and sunk on the *African Star* off the coast of South America and had spent four days at sea in a lifeboat before being rescued. He was given a month's leave in Rio de Janeiro, which he thought was great, but the terror was indelible. Henri's harrowing tales and his own close call with another torpedo on a voyage to Greenland made Jack very cautious. He told me he wanted to be very careful now that we were married. We spoke with the purser and watched the board for a couple of hours while hanging around with the seamen listening to their scuttlebutt.

Jack wanted to go for a beer at a waterfront saloon he called "Billy Bones." It was a big barn of a place, open to the weather with game machines all over. There was even a bucking bronco and a life-size gypsy doll in a glass booth that would tell your fortune for a quarter. The American flag hung in a prominent place with a fan that made it wave. Faded black and white pictures of Indians like Cochise, Crazy Horse and Sitting Bull adorned the walls. Billy Bones made you feel you were out West. Jack got two beers and we sat down at an old rickety table where we decided to have some lunch, since Billy Bones had great Boston baked beans and hot dogs. You bought a plate for thirty-five cents and helped yourself. First you put the dog on a bun and then added beans, cheese, chopped raw onions, mustard and catsup on top. Recalling our earlier visit to Billy Bones one Sunday on our way to an opening of my old art professor George Grosz's paintings with Joan, Celine, Lucien and Bill Burroughs, we wondered if Burroughs had gone back to St. Louis. After we finished, we returned our empty plates to the end of the bar and left.

We went back to the union hall where about a hundred men and women were gathered in small groups drinking wine, all talking at once. Jack and I joined in. We were handed a couple of glasses of cheap red wine, bitter and watery. A large homely woman who looked somewhat like Tug Boat Annie banged a gavel on the table to try to bring order. Annie spoke of the good work everyone was doing by taking food baskets to the widows of men lost at sea and by visiting hospitals where others were recuperating. A Russian woman spoke about herself and her shipmates sailing the high seas in a Swedish schooner. Then the chairperson asked if there were any new enlistments. I held up my hand, along with two others. We walked to the front of the hall and were sworn in. I was now an official member of the Women's Auxiliary Corps of the merchant marine as a Third Class Able Bodied Seaman. All the women hoped to ship out, but it was never to be. The meeting was adjourned and we were invited to attend a smaller meeting the following week at a Park Avenue apartment. Jack wrote down the address and time.

When we got home Jack took the dog out while I pitched in to help with supper and we talked about Nin's upcoming visit. She was older than Jack by a few years, but had already been married once and divorced. Now she was doing her part in the W.A.C.S. for the war effort. Gabe said she wanted to take Nin to the Village and have dinner at Jack Delaney's. "Nin likes that place. We all do, right? Me too," Gabe added with her French accent that flavored her statements. She told me that Nin's husband, Paul, was an MP in the army and was stationed in Alaska. In her letters, Nin wrote about how Paul loved Alaska and how he wanted to settle there, which they later did. She planned to arrive tomorrow by train from D.C., but we weren't going to meet her at the station, since we had no idea what time she'd get in.

That night after dinner, we all sat in the living room to listen to *Fibber McGee and Molly* and *Burns and Allen* on the radio, but they bored me, so I went into our bedroom and put on some Glenn Miller while I finished reading John O'Hara's *Pipe Night*. Jack came in around ten and turned the radio down as he got into bed. We held each other and talked about our plans to go to Michigan, where we could find work. We talked about Paris and the future when Jack would study at the Sorbonne. Maybe we'd even go to Hollywood where Jack could write for

Jack Kerouac and his sister Caroline (Nin) at the beach.

the movies. He thought it was a great way to write and be paid well for it. In those days there was opportunity in the movie studios, it was still wide open. After that we would be able to afford to move to Paris. Somehow in our dreams and fantasies we never considered the war or the fact that Paris was still occupied by the Nazis. We made love and fell asleep with a satisfied sigh, dreaming of the future.

chapter 30

. . .

When we woke, Gabe had already left for work. She left a long list of things for us to do and groceries to pick up. After we dressed and had our breakfast, Jack and I went to buy vegetables, meat and some fresh flowers, gladiolas as I recall. It was a real struggle for us to carry it all home on the bus, but once home, it was a joy to begin preparing that night's dinner. Jack helped by washing the vegetables. We put flowers all over. Besides the gladiolas, I had bought one white orchid, which I floated in a bowl on the table. Gabe said the place looked "spiffy" when she saw it. As I cooked, Jack worked on an article for the *Saturday Evening Post* about a huge fish, a fishing boat and a strange crew. Their boat sank and they were all in life boats and somehow this fish saved them all. I also remember sending the same story to *Redbook* magazine just before we left for Michigan. Jack had also submitted an article to *Colliers* about college football and what goes on behind the scenes. We hadn't heard from them yet or *Esquire* either, where Jack had sent a story about a young, sensitive athlete growing up in a small mill town. It told of the divide between his rough, tough friends and his intellectual, sensitive, poet friends and the inner conflicts that came from those two poles. I loved that story. We both wrote a lot of letters in those few days in Queens. Mine were to Joan telling her of our plans to go to Detroit and work in a factory. I promised her that I would send her money for the utility bills once she received them. I suggested we rent a third place, a larger one to accommodate her new baby, when we came back to New York. I guessed that we'd be back in three months at the most. Living with Gabe and Leo wasn't as bad as I'd anticipated, I said, and that Nin was coming to put her stamp of approval on my being "Jackie's" new wife. "That's what Gabe calls him . . . isn't that a riot?" I wrote. I also wrote to my Grosse Point friend, Jeanne Milner, telling her when we would arrive. I hoped my friends there would accept Jack.

Just then, out of nowhere, Nin walked in. She was about the same height as Jack, but a bit dumpy, like Gabe. Her personality was very cheerful, though, and the whole room brightened up the moment she walked in. She spoke in breathless tones, almost too deep for a girl. Her eyes were piercing and alert and her hair was short, black and curly. She came over to me at the table and gave me a kiss. "So, you're my new sister?" she asked. I felt a little embarrassed, but I liked her at once. "You married this big lug? Well, good luck! Mom has spoiled him rotten," she said. I was surprised because I had never thought that about Jack. I think she felt he should have been kicked out of the nest and forced to go to work. She probably felt that writing was not a very good way to make a living. Jack took that kind of abuse from every corner. His mother and I were the only ones who had faith in his talent. "Well, well. Here I am back in Mom and Dad's lap. Where is Pop anyway?" Nin asked. "Where else, the track," I said, "and of course mom is working." I told her we were just writing letters to Michigan to warn them of our coming. Nin suggested we try D.C. because there were lots of jobs available down there. Actually, we would have preferred to stay in New York, but my mother was alone and needed me. We also hoped to be able to save a little by living rent free and finding work in defense factories. Nin agreed with our plans and said that with our room and board taken care of, we'd have it made. I prepared some iced coffee to go with Gabe's brownies, and we sat at the kitchen table and talked.

Nin and I thought alike, but she would sometimes put Jack down. Not so much by what she said, but by her attitude toward him. It seemed to be a little more than a big sister thing, yet her put downs were subtle, like Leo's. I thought she had that "get a job" look in her eye. She would say things like, "Aren't you glad you tied the knot? Now things will work out for you, Jackie. You have a family to think about now. No more single life and vagabond dreams. You'll be knuckling down to the grindstone like the rest of us." She made both of us very uncomfortable at times. With the next breath she told me she loved my long curly hair. Since she was a WAC, she had to wear hers short, and she would have given anything for long hair and a sexy dress. When we started chattering about clothes, Jack got up and went into the bedroom and before long we could hear him hammering away at the typewriter.

"Don't you wish he was that dedicated to a real job?" Nin asked. When I got up from the table to take the dishes to the sink, Nin could tell I was a little peeved. I told her I liked the fact that Jack was a writer. Then she switched the subject to movie stars and her own experiences in Hollywood.

During the war, movie stars opened their homes to service personnel. Nin told me about meeting Lon McCallister* once at his home in Beverly Hills. She spoke to him about the chances of Jack working as a script synopsis writer in New York for M.G.M. and Twentieth Century Fox. Lon told her to send Jack out to Hollywood where there were plenty of opportunities since so many writers were in the service. She told McCallister that Jack was in the merchant marine, but could choose when he wanted to sail, and maybe have six months between each trip to sea to write. I didn't respond to her, letting her remark ride, but I knew the truth.

Leo came home and was thrilled to find Nin there. They hugged and kissed and decided to go out for a late lunch to get caught up. I could hear Jack still typing in the bedroom, so I took Woof-it out for her walk. Later, Nin and Leo returned from their lunch, Jack emerged from the bedroom, and we all began to talk about that evening. "Jack, what has Mom planned?" Nin asked. He said Gabe wanted to go to a favorite restaurant in Times Square and maybe take in a French movie. "Do you think she would go see Jean Gabin again in that imitation Camille flick? We've seen it twice already," I suggested.

---

* Lon McCallister was an actor who starred in movies of the late 1940s such as *The Big Cat* and *The Red House*.

"Probably, we can't disappoint her you know," Nin said. "Ma is very childish."

"Yeah," Jack said, "What a pain."

I suggested we all lighten up, for we were supposed to be having a good time. "It's our honeymoon, Jack!" I reminded him. He smiled from one side of his mouth, put his arm around my shoulder, gave me a kiss on my cheek and agreed. Nin left the table to unpack while I cleaned up the dishes.

Once Gabe came home from work we got ready to go into the city. On the bus to the subway station, Nin and Gabe sat together and talked, as did Jack and I. Leo always sat near the bus driver to talk with him, which I thought was a small town thing. Once on the subway we said very little. Jack sat across from me, his white shirt open at the neck. He was so handsome and shy that it seemed unreal to me. When he smiled and came over to lean down to kiss me, my heart and breath stopped out of sheer love. He took my hand and pulled me to my feet, grabbing me around the waist to steady me as the train lurched to a stop. Gabe watched us intently, but she was good at hiding her inner feelings.

As we left the train and walked along the platform to the exit, there was a fine mist falling through the sidewalk grates above on Times Square. Up the stairs to Broadway and around the corner, we found the Rathskeller, Gabe's favorite place. It was so crowded that we had to wait for a table while we dodged the umbrellas of all the people in the crammed vestibule. After a short wait, we were seated at a booth. The band was really going at it, playing the Beer Barrel Polka. They had the whole place singing, and Gabe and Leo joined right in. Nin, Jack and I were embarrassed and lip-synched the words instead. Everyone ordered knockwurst with sauerkraut, German potatoes and large steins of beer.

The place was filled with Times Square characters: there were men dressed in black suits with loud plaid vests, silk shirts and gold chains that held gold watches in their vest pockets. The women wore tight dresses or feminine suits of velvet with flashy jewels. They held long, fancy cigarette holders. You couldn't help but be fascinated by their jargon, which was right out of a Damon Runyon novel. Actors from a Broadway play filled one table. There were not many plays on Broadway during the war. Sometimes women had to play the men's roles and they were generally not well received by the public. I noticed there were no servicemen in the restaurant, only Nin was in uniform. The bartender, who Leo knew, told him that most of them were called back to their bases because an alert had been sounded.

When the band played you couldn't hear yourself talk. After dinner Gabe gave Leo enough money to pay the check and we left. We strolled around Times Square and read the news in the lights on the ticker, mostly news about the war punctuated by reminders to buy U.S. war bonds. Jack told me to take a good look at it all, because it would be a while before we'd see Times Square again. We both hated the thought of moving to Detroit; we thought of New York as our chosen home and where we wanted to be. Gabe and Leo wandered into one of the nickelodeons there, filled with games along the walls. Jack especially liked a game which pitted the Yankees against the Detroit Tigers, and he always wanted the Tigers to win. All the men got excited and loud, it was more thrilling than the real thing, and all for just a nickel! We, the girls, played the

The Kerouac family (Jack, Nin, Gabe and Leo) having a night on the town in New York.

pinball machines which tended to tilt at the slightest jar and would force you to put in another nickel. Jack adored these places. They were all over Times Square and in several other spots around the city as well. He and Leo played for over an hour that night until we grew bored waiting for them. Finally, they decided to quit in time to go see a movie.

Beau Geste with Gary Cooper, Ray Milland, Susan Hayward and Robert Preston was playing at the 42nd Street Playhouse. It had just opened, which was great, but it cost a dollar since it was a first-run movie. It was a great film about Tangier, the Casbah and the romantic side of war, and showed exotic places, gorgeous uniforms and beautiful women. Jack seemed very absorbed by anything about Arab culture and the Far East. After the movie he was quiet, deep in thought. For some reason the films in those days stayed with you for hours, not like today. We'd even find ourselves imitating the characters and their dialogue.

It was well after midnight by the time we got home. I helped Nin make her bed on the couch before going to our room. I could hear Leo snoring softly in the distance and Gabe humming her little French songs as she put her hair up for bed. Both her children were home and tomorrow was Sunday. In her world, all was well. The house was silent as I went to sleep beside my love.

The smell of coffee brewing and people talking woke me the next morning. Jack was still asleep beside me with KitKat curled in a ball at his feet. I was staring at the ceiling, reliving our last day and thinking about our future, until Jack woke up. He smiled and reached for me, giving me a good morning kiss. I got up, put Gabe's old robe on over my skimpy summer nighty, stretched a bit, and went to take a bath. Everyone, except Jack, was already up and waiting by the time I sat down at the kitchen table for some coffee and juice. They were talking about money. Gabe wanted Nin's allotment check, something Nin was loathe to give her since she needed what little she received for her own expenses. In addition, she was trying to put some of the money into war bonds to build a nest egg for when she got out of the service. I sided with Nin completely. Leo and Gabe had jobs, but Gabe always wanted more. Jack and Leo could not see anything wrong in her reasoning, but Nin and I sure did. I wondered whether Gabe would give Nin her paycheck if the circumstances were switched. I doubted it. The subject was dropped and I finished my coffee. When Jack came to the table, I tried to get back to the discussion about money. I didn't like the fact that Jack gave Gabe his allotment check either. I felt we needed to build our own nest egg for our future home when this was all over, not to support

Gabe's good times. But as I said, Jack wouldn't hear of it. As a result the morning breakfast that Sunday was rather glum, but Gabe's buckwheat pancakes soon put us all in a better mood.

chapter 31

. . .

Since Jack and I were married, we would be leaving soon for
Grosse Pointe. In spite of whatever arrangement he had with
his mother, Jack was anxious to get going. The fact that he
owed my mother money was weighing on his mind. He was
resigned to going to Michigan to get a job and pay her back,
and wrote her a letter telling her of his intentions. The following Monday we were on a train bound for Detroit. During the
war the trains were always crowded, especially during holidays
and this was Memorial Day, so we had to sit in the baggage
car for most of the trip with our pets. There was even a soldier's casket covered with an American flag.

When we arrived we were picked up by a car that had been
sent by my mother. She wasn't happy about our marriage or
the circumstances surrounding it, but decided to make the

best of it. She even gave us our own room at her house on Somerset.

Though my parents were divorced I was still close to my father, and he agreed to help Jack find a job. He made some calls and got Jack work at the Fruehauf Trailer Company inspecting ball-bearings on the midnight shift. He liked the fact that he had plenty of time to write and read the books he borrowed from the library. He called it the best job he ever had. Every payday he gave my mother some money, and by the end of the month he had paid her back. I was working too, at Chrysler's as a riveter.

We got word one day from New York that Lucien had plead guilty to second degree manslaughter. This meant Jack would not be called as a witness and the court decided to drop the charges against him. You can't imagine the load this took off our minds.

Jack was getting letters from his mother constantly. She would tell him how much she missed him and couldn't get used to the idea that she'd lost her son. She reminded him that they had left Lowell and moved to New York to be near him. My mother owned a shoe store, Ground Gripper Shoes, and this made Jack think of his own mother, her sacrifices, and her hard, long hours working in a shoe factory. On top of it, he had a hard time relaxing and felt he just didn't fit in in Grosse Pointe.

He felt the same way at Horace Mann because the other students came from money. When he wasn't working he was either sleeping or barricading himself in the bathroom for hours at a time reading Shakespeare and the Bible. He wore old clothes and didn't shave, and my friends did nothing to help him feel any better. To them he was out of place in Grosse Pointe. Once in a while my father would take us out on Lake St. Clair in his boat, which Jack loved, but that didn't make much difference. The one place where Jack felt at home was at the Rustic Cabin, a local bar on Kercheval.

By the end of September, Jack was already making plans to go back to New York and ship out with the merchant marine. He said there wasn't enough "tragedy" for him in Grosse Pointe. My mother even tried to talk to him about her favorite writer, Pearl Buck, but it did nothing to change his feelings. Things with us were good, but Jack needed to be

STUDENT SLAYER SENT TO THE REFORMATORY

Lucien Carr, the 20-year-old Columbia University engineering school student who last August confessed the slaying of David Kammerer, 33, former teacher of English and physical education in Washington University, St. Louis, was sentenced yesterday in General Sessions to Elmira Reformatory for first-degree manslaughter. He had stabbed Kammerer, a homosexual, on the embankment of Riverside Park at 115th Street, and had confessed the killing to the police more than twenty-four hours before the body was found floating in the Hudson River on Aug. 16.

Judge George L. Donnellan in imposing the sentence said he felt there was a chance for the rehabilitation of young Carr by sending him to the reformatory rather than to Sing Sing, where he could not avoid coming in contact with hardened criminals. The court warned him, however, that, while it would be possible for the youth to obtain his freedom from the reformatory in eighteen months, he would be shifted to Sing Sing to serve a possible fifteen-year term if he did not comply with the reformatory regulations.

Assistant District Attorney Jacob Grumet told the court that because the knife used in the killing had not been recovered by the police and there was no eyewitness, a second-degree murder conviction could not be obtained. Carr, who had been indicted for second-degree murder, pleaded guilty on the manslaughter charge.

where he felt secure. And I needed the security of having someone to take care of me. We still talked about going to Paris to live in Montparnasse after the war, but who knew when that might be.

Jack decided it was time to go, and Dad found him a free ride on a truck back to New York. When he got back he caught a ship, but that didn't last long either. One of the crew made a pass at him, and Jack was so upset he jumped ship in

Norfolk. You can't just leave your duty during a war, so he wound up being blacklisted and never got another ship. I found out he had made his way back to New York from Norfolk, but he didn't tell me or his mother at the time. I later found out he was living in Warren Hall near Columbia and working on his first book, *The Town and the City*. I had spoken with Celine and she told me he tried to seduce her, but she wasn't having any of it.

The whole time I thought he was overseas. I even got a letter from Gabe encouraging me to be patient with his trying to be a writer. I didn't hear from him until close to Christmas, and decided then to go back to New York to be together again. Joan, with her baby Julie, had managed to find another apartment at 419 W. 115th Street. Jack and I weren't there long before Allen and Bill moved in. To help share the rent, Hal Chase had also moved in as a boarder and got involved with Celine, I suspect because he looked something like Lucien. I didn't think he had Lucien's fire, though. He was very quiet but did strange things like hanging mirrors on the ceiling and stealing our food from the refrigerator. Joan had to put a lock on it to stop him. He wasn't very much like us but somehow blended in.

Around that time, Jack started talking about getting an annulment because he was no good as a husband. But I felt maybe he was going through a phase. In January I decided to go back home for a while. While I was there I was in a terrible car accident. I was thrown through the windshield of a car and nearly died from being cut up so bad. Jack came through a blizzard to see me, but once he knew I would be okay he went back to New York.

After I recovered I went back to the apartment in New York. I found a job as a cigarette girl at a place called the Zanzibar in Times Square from 7 P.M. to 4 A.M. six nights a week for $27.50. Jack and Bill would come down to visit me once in a while because I could occasionally finagle getting them a free steak dinner. Sometimes I smuggled the steaks out under my coat and brought them home for everybody. Jack and Bill would hang out having coffee at Bickford's, discussing anything and everything. That's where they first met Herbert Huncke while they were waiting for me to get off work.

I was the only one working, and most of the time we were eating mayonnaise sandwiches. Everyone was drinking more and Bill's new friend, Huncke, introduced drugs into the scene. Jack called it a year of "low, evil decadence." He talked more about getting a divorce, and I suspected there was someone

Hal Chase, Jack Kerouac, Allen Ginsberg and William Burroughs on Morningside Drive, winter 1944–45.

else. By May the situation with Jack and the wear of working to support everyone and the whole scene pushed me over the edge. I left and went to live with my grandmother at her house in Asbury Park for the summer.

Joan and Celine came to visit a couple of times, and one time Jack came along with Joan. We all went to the beach and Joan and I dressed Jack up with seashells and earrings and passed him off as a gypsy. I got a really bad sunburn, and Jack went off to buy some Noxzema to try and help. He also brought back some condoms and suggested we go to a motel. I thought maybe he was trying to reconcile with me but he just wanted to get laid. He was so drunk that after we made love he passed out and I left him there and went home to my grandmother's. I was more angry than I had ever been before with him.

In August Celine came to visit for a long weekend to try to help me figure it all out. She told me that she had run into Jack at the West End, and he had asked her to invite me to a party he was planning. Celine told him to ask me himself, but apparently Jack was too proud to be the first to call. Celine said to him, "Do you think you'll ever find another woman who understands you as well as Edie?" Jack never called, and by the end of September I helped my grandmother close up the house for the season and went back to Michigan.

My mother pressured me constantly to divorce Jack, telling me that I wasn't married or single. She said, "If you wait too long, things will get mixed up again." I still loved Jack, but I began to believe it was over. Then on September 18, 1946, I filed papers for an annulment.

For the next few years I didn't hear much from Jack. He was

off now with his friend, Neal Cassady. He wrote to Neal at the time, "My wife, if not Edie again, will be someone like her . . . wild . . . crazy . . . etc. . . . rushing off to mad bars, yet at the same time a sunny housekeeper."

In February of 1949, Jack got off a bus in Toledo and hitched a ride to Detroit to see me. By then my mother was remarried to the heir to the Berry Paint Company fortune, Joseph Sherrard. His father had worked with Henri Ford to develop the paint used for Ford automobiles. At that time we all lived in his Grosse Pointe Farms mansion at 59 Lakeshore Drive on Lake St. Clair. I had enrolled in college again at Michigan State to study horticulture and wasn't home when Jack called to say he was in town, so Jack had nowhere to go. For an hour on the phone he begged for my mother's help and asked her for a few dollars since he was broke. Finally he gave up and went to the bus station downtown and caught the next bus back to New York.

We spoke after he got back, and he said he hoped I would come back to New York to finish college. He was talking again about going to Europe, but now he said he wanted us to go to Italy on the advance money he got for *The Town and the City*. He wanted to learn to speak Italian like James Joyce and visit Joyce's Trieste. After that, we could go to Paris and live a life of leisure on his royalties, he said. But it was only a dream.

chapter 32

Jack did return to Detroit one more time to see me on a trip with Neal in September 1949. He and Neal had gotten a 1947 Cadillac limousine from a travel bureau in Denver that needed to be driven to Chicago. From there they decided to take a bus to Detroit. They stayed with me and my girlfriend, Virginia Tyson, at her parents' home in Grosse Pointe. Virginia's father, Ty Tyson, the Detroit Tigers' radio announcer, was out of town. I couldn't put them up at my house due to my mother, who didn't like Jack and his friends at all by that time. Jack was happy though, because he loved the grand piano in Virginia's sunken living room, and Neal was attracted to Virginia.

Virginia wanted to have a big party since she had the run of the house. Her brother Billy was at home, but he was no problem; he had his own crazy group of friends. Virginia decided to

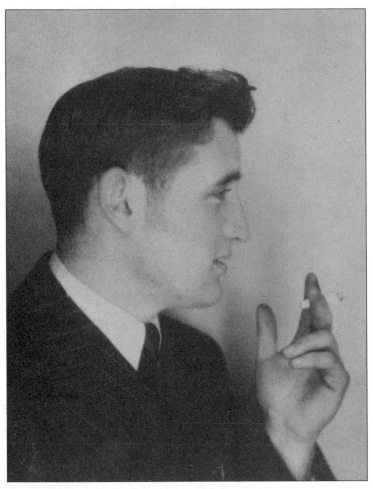

Neal Cassady's photo booth portrait.

have the party catered, so we went shopping and spent everything we had on booze and big roasts. Thank God for her charge accounts, or she would have dined on cookies for the next two months. One advantage was that the house was stocked with cases of all the products her father advertised, including beer.

As I saw it, Jack and I had not conventionally "split up." In a manner of thinking, we never really did. We were just caught up in the excitement of our lives, of what we were doing from day to day, enjoying the freedom of finally having become adults, and after a while our parents left us pretty much alone. My mother was pleased that I was back in Grosse Pointe, out of New York for good, and thought that Jack was out of my life, which could not have been further from the truth.

Jack and Neal arrived by Greyhound from Chicago in the middle of the day. We stuck their canvas luggage in the trunk and off we went, Neal in the driver's seat with Virginia and Jack and I holding hands tightly in the backseat. We loved each other and I could see he was happy traveling. "Go" as John Clellon Holmes' book says. The top was down on the big white Lincoln convertible, the radio was blaring, and we were all talking at the same time. The wind was in our sails, whoo-whee!

First we stopped at the Rustic Cabin saloon for drinks. Since Virginia drank V.O. and ginger ale, we all did, even though we had a tough time rounding up the cash between us. Funny thing about Grosse Pointers: they have everything except cash! When Jack got back from the men's room he was grinning and he ordered another round, producing a crumpled up ten spot. Neal was shocked. "Where did you get that gold?" he asked. Jack never answered. Neal didn't know Jack as well as I did. Jack gave Neal a quarter for the great jukebox. Pete Ouelette, the French Canuck owner of the bar, loved Frank Sinatra, so Neal played six of Sinatra's songs for two bits and we had to sit through all of them.

We got to Virginia's about four and found Billy playing baseball in their big front yard. Jack and Neal joined right in with the gang, Neal pitching, Jack catching. A friend of Billy's came over and helped Virginia and me with the luggage. We put Neal in the room with the double bed, and Jack in the twin-bedded master bedroom. The house had four bedrooms and four huge bathrooms.

Virginia and I unpacked their luggage and asked her maid Maggie to do the laundry. Maggie was cooking dinner with her daughter downstairs in the kitchen. Some great smells were drifting through the house: hams, turkeys, potato salad, and garlic meat sauce for the spaghetti.

The Tysons dined at seven by candlelight, and Jack was expecting the same treatment. It had been the custom at my mother's house, too. Suddenly the piano came alive, Jack was playing loud jazz music. Neal wanted a beer, which was through the kitchen and outside, so I showed him where the cupboards were, filled with cases of Altes beer, Wheaties, cookies, and Chuckles candies. All items Tyson helped advertise.

Ty Tyson had a live broadcast called "The Man On the Street," where he talked to people impromptu in front of the Michigan Central Railroad Station every day at noon for station WWJ. Eventually he became president of the station. Ty always wore a black French beret; one was even placed on his casket when he died, and his pallbearers wore them. I also wore one as a hostess for that memorable event. All the Detroit sports and political big shots came to the house for Ty's wake; it was the same kind of wonderful party we gave for Jack and Neal the next day.

Virginia was nervous, so she kept all the silver locked away in drawers. She didn't have to worry, for Neal would never have done anything to discredit Jack. If Neal had been alone, however, she would have had more than silver to worry about! As seven o'clock approached, Jack went upstairs to take his customary shower and shave. He came back downstairs wearing one of Billy's clean white shirts without a tie. Jack scowled at Neal, so he went to wash up and comb his hair, too.

We enjoyed a delicious dinner and brought our plates to the kitchen afterwards, rinsing them and setting them in the sink. Then Virginia served coffee, apple pie, and Sander's vanilla ice cream. That was Jack's favorite dessert, so he was pleased. Neal wanted to know whose birthday it was! He was always making corny remarks.

In the living room Jack and I stretched out on the floor by the fire. Virginia and I didn't know what to do about the music for the party—we thought we could either play the radio or play our own records on the Victrola. Jack and Neal said to leave it to them and they'd take care of the music. Then we all went to bed. After a long day, Jack and I were anxious to be together again behind closed doors.

The next day flew by fast. Jack, Billy and Neal went to see about a getting a band. While they were gone I was so excited about Jack's return that I started drinking too much, too soon. When the guests arrived, I was well on my way. We held the party in the Tyson's rathskeller, a finished basement with a bar that had Altes beer on tap. We put a large assortment of food on the covered ping-pong table. Jack and Neal had found a black, three-piece band—where, I'll never know. They were great, with Jack and Neal taking turns on the drums. They also played an old upright piano. We drank and danced late into the night; it was wonderful. By midnight, I was exhausted and went to bed. I woke up once to hear the party still going strong and heard Jack finally come to bed when it was light. As he crawled into my twin bed, I heard the musicians laughing and leaving in a cab. Then I fell back to sleep.

I got up before the rest of the crowd and put on my pajamas. After making some coffee I set about cleaning and picking up the glasses, slowly working my way downstairs. Then one of the guests got up and reported that the toilets were stopped up, so I phoned the plumber for emergency repairs. The plumbers arrived and went all over the house with electric snakes and other paraphernalia looking for the clog. It took them a half day to discover that the problem was in the main sewer pipe under the front lawn. In the meantime, some of the guests were still partying, particularly Neal. I wondered who he'd slept with. When I woke Virginia to tell her about the plumbing situation, she put me in charge and went right back to sleep.

In the end the plumbers had to dig up the front yard to fix it. Someone had flushed a pair of men's shorts down the drain, they were white with big red polka dots! We became hysterical with laughter when we saw them. Fortunately, no one claimed them, but later Jack wrote me that they had been Neal's.

The plumbers mended everything just as before, except for the new bump in the lawn which made it look like someone was buried there. When Virginia got the bill it was for more than the cost of the entire party. She was furious.

Well, the party went on for days, then everything ran out: beer, food, patience and hospitality. Jack and Neal had to move to the Saverine Hotel, a favorite of the Detroit Tigers baseball players. Since they really didn't have any money anyway, Virginia used her connections to get them a discount room, which she and I later paid for. So they enjoyed the rest of their stay with the Tigers at the Saverine, with fun players like Roy Cullenbine, Barney Markowsky, and Dick Wakefield.

One afternoon we were drinking beer, and then we changed to Courvoisier brandy. That was when Lee and I discovered Manhattans made with that brandy were delicious. Then Clot, Neal, Jack, Tyne and a few others started playing baseball in the yard. This time Jack played right field, Neal was pitcher, Clot played second base, Tyne was catcher, Lee took third, and I covered first base! It was hilarious, none of us were "feeling any pain," and the game did not last long. Then Tyne suggested we eat. We had a ball sitting on that wonderful porch, looking out at beautiful Lake St. Clair. Jack wrote about it all in *On the Road*, but his editor, Malcolm Cowley, cut out most of what he wrote of his Detroit visits and changed the name of Lake St. Clair to Lake Michigan, which is clear across the state from Grosse Pointe.

[end of Edie's narrative]

chapter 33

as told to the editor

. . .

After three wild days in Michigan, Jack and Neal pressed on to New York in a new 1949 Chrysler, arriving there in late August. After that visit Edie and Jack drifted apart as the years passed. They each went their separate ways. From time to time Jack would write or call Edie. The calls often came late at night when he was quite drunk, but Edie always spent time talking with him. In 1957 after reading of the publication of *On the Road*, Edie spoke with Jack who was staying at the Marlton Hotel in New York at the time. He told her that he still dreamed of her and loved her in his own way. In a letter he wrote a few days later he explained to her his Buddhist ideas and signed the letter as "your eternal old man, Jack."

More and more, Jack became a victim of his alcoholism. He

became abusive of his friends on the telephone and one by one, they refused to take his calls. Most of his calls to old girlfriends like Helen Weaver, Helen Eliot, Lois Sorrels and Edie were romantic reminiscences of times gone by. He continued to write, and the story of his rise as a novelist and fall as a man is told in many biographies. Edie remained in Grosse Pointe for the rest of her life and married two more times. One of her husbands was a golf pro and the other was a used car salesman, but neither marriage lasted. When Edie's mother died their house was sold and the money was put in a trust fund for Edie and her sister. Occasionally Jack would call and one of her husbands would answer the phone. That invariably led to Jack's angry warnings to get out of his wife's bed.

Then in September of 1969, Edie received a long letter from Jack. They had been talking about getting together in Detroit for a reunion, but Jack had just been beaten up in a barroom fight, receiving stitches after he was taken to jail. "So I am too sick to go to Detroit," he wrote. "All black eyes and blue arms and stitches over eye (4) and twisted knee. So if you want to see me (and my mother and I both want to see you) get a roundtrip ticket to here and come have pleasant quiet visit. By bus if necessary. Expect no money from me on any scale, I'm not rich like you think. But the house is a beaut, the yard has a fenced in grass, shrub, tree and jungled area: there's a screened porch. Walk to store. Hurricane proof Spanish modern CASTLE, which explains where all my money went. Come on down, therefore, and we'll hash out whatever future there is. Stella is from Lowell, she's the sister of that young Greek soldier Sebastian who died at Anzio beach head in 1943. She won't like it but come on down anyway. No moochy

moochy. For some reason my Ma (paralyzed in bed but still funny) wants to have you visit. And I don't mind at all because I'd like to talk over things and all old times with you. Relax and be calm. Tell your DuPonts lend you fare, for krissakes. Jack. P.S. And don't you dare bring anyone else or any dogs or cats or any animals. I've got 3 quiet happy cats, beauts, and plenty peaceful area (svelte)."

With Gabe's consent, Jack sent a brief telegram to Edie a few weeks later, restating his invitation for her to come to Florida to visit them. "Have money available for air fare. Own here. So forget that job and come quick as you can. Jack Kerouac."

However on September 21, 1969, soon after sending the telegram, he wrote to her that he, his mother and Stella had all decided that she should not visit. "Dear Edith," he wrote, "My mother, my wife, and I, myself have decided you should not come here at all. You would not enjoy it here anyway, with a paralytic patient under 24-hour care. There is no room to put you up in, and I am so busted (hernia) that I can't see straight, or walk straight, or think logically. Cancel the message in the telegram and try to go see your friend, Milner in California. Bad time for both of us. Jack. You'll be Okay."

Jack was to die exactly a month later, on October 21, 1969, of complications brought on by his alcoholism. After the funeral, Jack's widow, Stella, wrote a friendly letter to Edie which ended, "take good care of yourself—when I married Jack, I thought I had finally reached the end of the rainbow— 'Who can see what lies before us, what of joy or what of woe. Who can see what fate has stored for us. Nay, tis well we do not know.' Keep the home fires burning, Edie. You and I are made from the same mold. We love not wisely but too well."

In 1982, Allen Ginsberg invited Edie to lecture at the Naropa Institute on the subject of her life with Jack Kerouac in honor of the twenty-fifth anniversary of the publication of *On the Road.* She prepared notes for those talks, and those expanded in the following years into this memoir. The last decade of her life was spent writing and lecturing on Kerouac. She received a degree in horticulture from Michigan State University and pursued her interest in plants and animals in her home in Detroit.

afterword
by timothy moran

· · ·

One morning in early June 1988, while I was leafing through Edie's copy of *The Kerouac Connection* that had just arrived in the mail, I came across an announcement for the June 25th dedication of the Jack Kerouac Commemorative in Lowell's Eastern Canal Park. There were to be five days of panel discussions, readings and tours, and all the big names would be there: Allen Ginsberg, Lawrence Ferlinghetti, Robert Creeley, Michael McClure and Ray Manzarek of *The Doors*. When I showed it to Edie she was surprised and upset that she'd not been contacted, so I called one of the organizers of the event. He seemed hesitant to provide me with any real specifics about the event, but assured me that not inviting Edie had been merely an oversight. He told me he would call back, but he never did, and with each passing day Edie grew more upset.

Edie Kerouac-Parker at her Detroit home, 1989.

As the time for the dedication drew nearer, I told Edie we should just go, invitation or not, even if we had to crash the festivities. I also suggested to her that we stop in New York City on the way from Detroit and pick up Henri Cru. She agreed and her disappointment immediately turned to excitement as we began planning our trip to Lowell via New York. That was the easy part. Convincing Henri to go along was a little more difficult.

By the time of Jack's death, Henri and Jack had become estranged from one another and time had not softened his contempt for what his best friend, Jack Kerouac, had become. "They just would not leave him alone," Henri later explained to me. "I went to see him and his mother a few times out in Northport, Long Island. His mother and I always got along terrifically, treated me like I was her own son. They had to have a tremendous, eight-foot fence put up around the house to keep out kids who would show up at all hours to take him out drinking and Jack could never say no to anybody. Man, his mother had a hell of a time. You know his mother used to give him money to come into the city. He'd come over to my place on MacDougal Street and we'd go have a few beers, but by then not one bar in Greenwich Village would serve him a drink unless I guaranteed to be responsible for him if he acted up. Once drunk he would begin insulting people and you just couldn't do that sort of thing. One time I saw him on Bleecker, where Jack yelled out at two big guys walking across the street, 'Hey, Henri, look at those two big fags!' Well, I knew he only said it because he was drunk, but those guys came over and busted him up. It took stitches to close his face back up. Another time I took a girlfriend of mine out to Northport, because I wanted to impress her by introducing her to my friend, the famous writer. When we got there Jack was already quite drunk. There was a picture of him on the table, the best one I've seen, taken at the Village Vanguard with the trombone player, J.J. Johnson, in the background. I asked him to sign it to her and he barely got through her name before he passed out face down on the kitchen table."

"His getting the local liquor store to send over two or three fifths of whiskey every day was the worst thing that ever happened to him," Henri continued. "It was Wilson's whiskey, and Wilson's was the bottom of the barrel. They all thought they were doing him a big favor." As time went by, even Henri couldn't put up with him. They last saw one another in the 1960s at a party at Dodie Mueller's apartment in the Village. I asked Henri if he had gone to Jack's funeral and he told me, "Well, I read that he had died, but what was I going to go up to Lowell for? I didn't have anything to say to him and I don't think he was going to say anything to me, either." It took half a dozen phone calls and a lot of coaxing before Henri finally relented and agreed to go with us to the dedication.

The day before we set out, I began getting nervous about all the luggage Edie had pulled down from the attic. I assumed that she was trying to decide which suitcase might be best for the trip, but the next morning every one of the suitcases—five in all—were lined up at the front door, packed and waiting for me to take out to the car. I hoped that was the end of it, but when I went back into the house Edie had stacked more things at the front door: paintings, papers, bags of books, and all sorts of paraphernalia. "What the hell is all this, Big E?" I asked.

"Well, Big T, you know I don't want to get there and discover I forgot something important," she explained. "Don't worry, it'll be all right." I told her it was my back that might not be all right, not to mention that we still had to fit Henri into the car. We had an eleven-hour drive ahead of us, and it was 9:00 A.M. by the time we hit the road. Once out of the rush-hour traffic, we hit I-75 and it was smooth sailing all the way to the Chelsea Hotel on West 23rd Street where we spent the night before picking up Henri. As I pulled up in front of the Chelsea, I realized I'd have to haul the entire contents of the car up to our room. Edie went inside and got the key while I unloaded everything into the lobby.

By 1988 the Chelsea had seen better days. The owner of the hotel, Stanley Bard, assured us that he was giving us one of his finest rooms, replete with a fireplace and kitchenette. When we got upstairs we noticed that he'd forgotten to mention that the room also came with a television with a state-of-the-art, wire coat hanger antenna on it and a complimentary mouse that came free with the room. Edie flopped down on one bed, while I finished moving in and then I crashed on the other. We lay exhausted and tried to watch a *Rockford Files* re-run through the dense snow of the television screen. We didn't stay up late. Henri was expecting us at 10:00 the next morning and I did not want to be late, as it was the first time I'd meet Henri in person.

Henri was living in the old Mills Hotel on Bleecker in the Village, and somehow Edie had neglected to tell me that Henri was confined to a wheelchair. He had lost his left leg to diabetes several years earlier. As we pulled up, Henri was sitting in his chair at the curb wearing an old Sorbonne t-shirt and a red Budweiser baseball cap. He had no luggage, just a small khaki-colored duffle bag secured with a brown leather belt around the middle. We got out to greet him and his first words were, "I hope you are going to have room to fit my wheelchair. That car looks like it doesn't have much of a trunk."

I assured him that everything would work out fine, but in my head I had no idea how it would fit. First I tried to get the chair into the back seat, but it wouldn't even clear the door opening. I began to fear that we would lose Henri even before we got started. Then I went back to the trunk and began emptying everything out all over Bleecker Street to the assault of angry car horns. Edie stood on the sidewalk like a loading dock foreman and barked directives as Henri sat in amused silence. Since there was just no way the wheelchair would fit into the trunk with all of Edie's belongings there, I began to pile Edie's things into the back seat. Finally I got the chair into the trunk and filled whatever space remained around it with her stuff. Because of all the crap on the back floor the passenger seat had to be as far forward as it would go, and since Henri was a large man there was little room for him. At one point I had to grab the seat cushion from his wheelchair and jam it between his stump and the dashboard, and he held his bag on his lap. Seeing no space left, Edie asked where she would sit. I pointed to the back seat, so she crawled in on her hands and knees and flipped onto her side on top of the luggage where she had to ride horizontally on top of everything she had insisted on bringing.

We certainly drew stares from the passersby as we pulled out. "Well, we made it. That certainly was some magic act you performed, Big Tim!" Henri laughed. "Isn't this fun, Henri? I told you it would be," Edie enthused. Henri looked at me, sighed and rolled his eyes.

It didn't take long for Edie to begin reflecting on the old days. She talked so fast that Henri could barely get a word in. "I can see not much has changed, Edith," Henri said as he grew frustrated. It had been more than forty years since they had last seen each other. A few years earlier, when Edie had decided to begin writing her memoirs, she had placed an ad on the back page of the *Village Voice* offering a reward of $100 to anyone who could put her in contact with Henri.

One of Henri's old friends saw it and told Edie that Henri was in Cabrini Hospital just about to undergo surgery to have his leg removed. She called at once, and when Henri answered the phone Edie asked, "Are you still pissed off at me, Henri?"

Henri responded, "I'm too old and seen too much to be angry anymore, Edith." Now, in the car together, it was as if they picked up right where they had left off, like it was only yesterday.

"Do you remember when you first introduced me to Jack, Henri?" Edie asked him.

"Remember?" said Henri. "We were walking down to a theater on 110th Street and encountered a few of Edith's friends, who all seemed pleasant enough. Well, Edie turns to introduce me and says, 'I would like to introduce you to my fiancée, Henri Cru.' I jumped about a foot off the sidewalk and yelled, 'YOUR WHAT?' She had some idea that since we were makin' it, we were engaged. Understand that I do not breed well in captivity, Big T. That is when I marched her over to the dorm to meet Jack." Their recollections about the past seemed largely at odds, but for me it was fascinating to just be there listening to them talk.

What should have been a five-hour drive became closer to eight. Henri was incontinent, which required us to stop at least every half hour. When we finally arrived in Lowell, Edie insisted we go directly to the cemetery to see Jack's grave. Our directions were completely dependent on her memory from her last visit of nineteen years earlier, so we drove all over town trying to find the Edson cemetery. By the time we did, Henri was hungry and out of patience, and he kept reminding me that his pal, "String Beans" had promised him a return bus ticket if he decided to go back early. I headed straight back to the center of town and pulled up in front of the Club Diner. There was no way Henri could get inside with his wheelchair so I asked what he and Edie wanted and went inside to get a take-out. We sat at the curb eating burgers and fries as evening fell.

Without a reservation for a place to stay we began cruising Lowell. Eventually we came across a small motel on the outskirts of town and pulled in for the night. Edie went into the office while Henri and I waited in the car. She got two adjoining rooms, one a double and the other a single. Of course, Edie took the double and gave Henri and me the single. While I unloaded Edie's things into her room, Henri settled into ours.

Several times during the drive up from New York, I had asked Henri what he had in his bag, but he would not tell me. When I came into the room, Henri had a big grin on his face. He had set two plastic cups on top of the television set, beside a warm 40 oz. bottle of Ballantine. That was his surprise and all that he had brought on the trip except for a red-and-white striped short-sleeve shirt. It was the only shirt he owned with a collar, and he wanted to have something nice to wear.

The next morning I got up early and went out while Henri was still sleeping. I found a beverage center and bought a case of beer and several bags of ice. Back in the

Henri Cru and Edie at Jack Kerouac's grave, 1988.

room I filled the bathtub about one third with cold water and dumped the ice and beer into it. When Henri woke and discovered it, he was thrilled. Before long Edie knocked on the door. She said there was a laundry room and she was going to wash her clothes and offered to wash ours too. I declined and warned Henri that back home Edie's attempts to wash my clothes had always resulted in most of them being turned into tie-dyed hand puppets. Since she insisted, Henri gave her his socks and T-shirt in spite of my warnings to the contrary. I took a walk to clear my head, but when I returned, I found all hell breaking loose. Edie had done the wash, but lost one of Henri's socks. "I knew I should have listened to you, Big Tim," he said. "Now what am I going to do!"

We all searched high and low and I went to check the machines in the laundry as a last resort. When I came back to our room Henri was red-faced and chuckling, "You'll never believe this, Big Tim. You know what happened to my sock? Nothing! There never was a sock—I've only got one foot! One foot—one sock." We all laughed hysterically.

That morning we went back to Edson Cemetery to visit Jack's grave. At least this time we knew where we were going. We were the only people there as I pulled up on the grass in front of the marker and got Henri into his chair. Edie was very quiet and only said, "Well, this is it, Henri." The grave is marked by an inscribed rectangular granite stone set flush to the ground and we stared down in silence for what seemed like ten minutes. Finally Henri reached into the green nylon bag hanging from the handles of his wheelchair and pulled out a bottle of wine, labeled, "Cheap Red Wine." He asked me to hand him a pen from the bottom of the bag and with tears filling his eyes, he inscribed it "From Your Pal, Henri Cru" and placed it on top of the stone. Then he pulled out a copy of the *Kerouac Connection* which featured an interview with him and his picture on the cover, signed it "Henri Edouard Cru," and put it on the tombstone beside the bottle.

"Can you feel him, Henri?" Edie asked. "Jack always told me he wanted to die," Henri said. "Said he didn't have the nerve to kill himself—thought drinking himself to death was glamorous—all the great writers drank themselves to death. The doctors told him if he stopped drinking he could live another fifteen years, if not, he'd be dead in six months. He didn't stop and he was dead in six months. He felt he'd never be taken seriously until he was dead."

Tim Moran, Edie, and Henri Cru in Lowell, Massachusetts, 1988.

Just then a yellow school bus filled with about twenty people out on a tour of Kerouac's Lowell pulled up. The last one off the bus was Jan Kerouac, Jack's only daughter. She immediately spotted Henri and came rushing over, "Hey Henri! What are you doing here? This must be Edie. Why don't you introduce me?" Henri just turned his head away as Edie and Jan introduced themselves and exchanged small talk.

Jan turned towards me and asked Edie, "Who's this, Edie? My half brother or something?"

"Oh God, no. This is Big Tim," she said. Years earlier, Henri had sent money regularly to Jan's mother, Joan Haverty, to help her out because Jack was not paying his child support. Henri told me that when Jack was dragged into court for non-payment, he denied to the judge that he was Jan's father. The judge laughed at him and told him that Jan looked more like him than he did and ordered him to pay up. When Jan got older Henri continued to send money to Jan whenever she asked for help.

"Boy, Henri, remember those great dinners you used to make for me when I stayed with you?" Jan said. "In *The Dharma Bums* my father wrote about having chicken soup and said it was the best he'd had since Henri Cru's chicken soup." But now, what was most on Henri's mind was the last hundred bucks he'd sent to Jan for a bus ticket, and she had put it to something else and never acknowledged the gift. By then Edie and Henri were tired and we headed back to the motel to rest.

That evening was to be the big reading of the event, held at the Smith Baker Center. It was to feature Ginsberg, Creeley, Ferlinghetti, McClure and Manzarek. Edie was all hyped up about it, but Henri was wearing down fast. Before we went to the Baker Center we stopped at the Owl Diner for some dinner—heaping plates of turkey on sliced white bread and smashed potatoes beneath ponds of thick yellow gravy. When we got to the auditorium, Edie went in while I found two parked cars on the side of the building where Henri could piss.

By the time we got inside, the place was packed and sold out. As I pushed Henri down the aisle to the front, people began whispering and wondering who this guy was. Edie overheard several of them and started calling out, "This is Henri Cru—Remi Boncouer!" No one seemed to know what to make of it. I sat down in the first row with Henri parked in the aisle beside me and Edie sat in the seat across the aisle. The crowd buzzed with anticipation trying to spot literary legends. Suddenly all heads turned as Allen Ginsberg made his way down the aisle from the back of the auditorium. Voices from the balcony called out to him as all eyes followed. Henri sat, oblivious to it all, until Allen came up from behind and put his arm around Henri's back while leaning down to kiss him on the cheek before going on stage. Anyone who didn't know who Henri was certainly would now.

He turned to me deliberately wiping his hand across his face, "I've told that guy before, I'm not into that stuff!" Throughout the reading Henri's head never rose and at times he dozed off. When Allen began reading *Howl* he spontaneously inserted Henri's name in one of the lines. As if touched by the healing hands of a T.V. minister, Henri's eyes suddenly sprang open. He really didn't know what had been said, he only knew he'd heard his name. From that point on everyone began approaching him knowing he had to be somebody special. I felt certain that this was what Allen had intended. Henri, who had been bitter and

Allen Ginsberg and Henri Cru, 1988.

hiding from prying Kerouacians for years, was suddenly feeling excited, though he wouldn't say so. I couldn't wait to see what would happen the next afternoon at the dedication of the memorial.

Edie was up with the dawn. Her emotions had kept her from sleeping most of the night and Henri was actually anxious to get there, too. He even had stopped threatening to call "String Beans" for the return ticket. After a leisurely breakfast back at the Owl, we headed over to the park. As we approached, we could see that the park was overflowing with fans, reporters and television cameras. Almost immediately Edie and Henri were besieged by the media and fans seeking a word or an autograph. They both loved it and caused such a commotion that it seemed like they might steal the show. I stepped away, staying within earshot if they needed me, while they basked in the limelight.

Before long, the official celebrants began to fill the dais. Allen was there, as well as Stella Sampas, Jack's widow, along with all the local and state politicians who until that moment had disavowed Jack's ties to Lowell. They thought of him as a drunkard and the town might be better off if they forgot about him entirely. The ceremony was all very dignified and stiff, and throughout it most of the crowd and media attention was focused on Henri and Edie, who ignored the official speeches.

When it was all over and the crowds began to disperse, I overheard someone telling Ferlinghetti about a party that was being thrown at one of the hotels for the guests. I went over to Edie and told her we should go and she said, "I don't know, Big T, maybe they don't want us to go. Nobody invited us." Henri wheeled his way over after giving an interview to a reporter from the *Lowell Sun* newspaper. We told him what was going on and asked him what he thought we should do. Just then, out of nowhere, a woman approached extending her hand and smiling. She said she was having a few people over to her house and asked if we would like to follow her there for some beer and pizza.

Henri didn't hesitate, "Beer and pizza? Sure, we'd love to!" She pointed to her car and said she would wait for us while I went for the car and picked up Edie and Henri. Then we were off, right behind our new friend who lived nearby. We arrived to find about a dozen people in her dining room, eating pizza and well into the beer. Henri seemed to fit right in and regaled them with his tales. Edie held back a bit, wondering what we were doing there and wishing she had been invited to the big shindig at the hotel. We stayed for quite a while and almost had to pry Henri out of there. By the time we got back to the motel that evening, it was Henri who was hyped up and Edie who had taken his blue mood.

When we got up the next morning Edie was anxious to be on her way, so we decided to get breakfast on the road. It was a beautiful, clear day and there was really no rush, but Edie wanted to go. I loaded up the car and we started out of town, but as we passed a news box Henri asked me to stop and get a paper. He suspected he might be mentioned in it, so I got him the paper and he skimmed through the pages. It didn't take long for him to find a full-page article featuring a picture of both he and Edie. By that time Edie was no longer interested in Lowell or the memorial and begged me to get going, but Henri interrupted her and put his foot down. "Now, Edith, I have gone along with everything you've asked. I came up here and I would like to take a little more time before we leave. Big Tim, I want you to do me a favor and go back to that box and get me every copy of the *Lowell Sun* in there. Then I want to drive around town a little bit and see if we can find some more."

We ended up covering almost every street in town and before it was over Henri had nearly fifty copies of the *Lowell Sun* stacked on the floor with his leg resting on top of them. The trip turned out to be the greatest thing he could have imagined and somehow it brought him to forget the feelings of the past he'd brought with him. It was as if the wounds of his last memories of Jack had healed. For Edie, the trip was a great disappointment and she hardly uttered a word on the way home. It seemed that the trip had robbed her of what she had hoped to reclaim in Lowell, and she came to realize that her life with Jack was past.

Edie Kerouac-Parker at her Detroit home, 1989.

update
. . .

JOAN VOLLMER ADAMS: Joan was drawn deeper into the world of benzedrine and at one point in 1946 was sent to the mental ward at Bellevue Hospital. She was rescued by William Burroughs, who became her common-law husband and fathered a son with her in 1947, William Burroughs, Jr., but substance abuse remained a problem. One night in 1951, Burroughs accidentally shot Joan in the forehead when she placed a glass on top of her head and asked William to shoot it off, *á la* William Tell. She was pronounced dead at a Mexico City hospital. Her daughter Julie was raised by her family in Loudonville.

G.J. (GEORGE) APOSTOLOS: Jack's childhood friend from Lowell, married and continued to live there for his entire life.

WILLIAM S. BURROUGHS: After William rescued Joan from the mental hospital, they relocated to Texas for the purpose of tending a marijuana farm. They moved on to New Orleans and Mexico City, where William accidentally killed Joan. He fled to North Africa and Europe, living there for the next thirty years. He began writing as a result of the murder and became acknowledged as one of the great novelists of the twentieth century. In 1983 he was inducted into the American Academy of Arts and Letters. He died in 1997, about four months after Allen Ginsberg's death.

LUCIEN CARR: After spending two years in the Elmira Reformatory, Lucien was released and went to work for the United Press International in New York. He stayed with U.P.I., retiring in the late 1980s from their Washington bureau. He spent his retirement in Washington, and enjoyed sailing on the Chesapeake Bay until his death in 2005. He married, had three children, one of whom is Caleb Carr, the author of the best-selling book, *The Alienist.*

NEAL CASSADY: Neal continued on the road for many years and lived an exuberant, fast-paced, drug-filled life. Many people believe he burnt himself out before he collapsed and died of exposure in Mexico in 1968, a year before Kerouac's death. His autobiographical fragment *The First Third* was published after his death.

HENRI CRU: For the most part, Henri Cru avoided the media attention placed on the Beat Generation and spent most of his life as a merchant seaman. He never married and died in Greenwich Village in 1991.

ALLEN GINSBERG: Allen went on to become one of the country's greatest poets. In 1956 he published his most famous poem "Howl," which has sold over a million copies. In 1972 he founded the Jack Kerouac School of Disembodied Poetics in Boulder, CO, where he taught for twenty years. He died in 1997 at the age of 70.

CAROLINE "NIN" KEROUAC: Jack's sister married Paul Blake, but died at the age of forty-five in 1964.

GABE KEROUAC: After suffering a stroke in 1966, Jack's mother outlived him and remained with Stella until her death in 1973. She outlived all three of her children.

STELLA SAMPAS KEROUAC: Jack married his third wife in 1966. Stella took care of Gabe Kerouac until she died four years after Jack in 1973. Stella herself passed away in 1990 in Lowell and is buried next to Jack.

CHARLOTTE PARKER (MOTHER): Edie's mother died in the early eighties, at which time Edie had to leave the family home.

CHARLOTTE PARKER PATTISON (SISTER): Edie's sister married shortly after the events of this story and moved to Massachusetts where she lives to this day.

SEYMOUR WYSE: Wyse continued to educate Jack about jazz and later moved to Europe where Kerouac visited him once on a trip to Paris. He returned to his native England and ran a record shop in London.

CELINE YOUNG: Celine married, had children and lost touch with her friends. Lucien Carr believed that she had passed away by the 1990s.

photo credits

. . .

p. 9: Copyright Timothy Moran

p. 24: Courtesy of the *New York Times*

p. 37: Photo by Edie Kerouac-Parker, copyright Timothy Moran, courtesy of the Allen Ginsberg Trust

p. 40: Copyright Timothy Moran

p. 52: Copyright Timothy Moran, courtesy of the Beats Collection: Edie Parker and Henri Cru Papers, Rare Book Collection, The Wilson Library, University of North Carolina at Chapel Hill

p. 59: Copyright Timothy Moran

p. 67: Copyright the Allen Ginsberg Trust

p. 74: Copyright the Allen Ginsberg Trust

selected bibliography
. . .

Charters, Ann. *Kerouac: A Biography.* San Francisco: Straight Arrow Books, 1973.

Clark, Tom. *Jack Kerouac.* NY: Harcourt Brace Jovanovich, 1984.

Kerouac, Jack. *Selected Letters 1940-1956.* Edited by Ann Charters. NY: Viking, 1995.

Kerouac, Jack. *Windblown World: The Journals of Jack Kerouac 1947-1954.* Edited by Douglas Brinkley. NY: Viking, 2004.

Kerouac Parker, Edie. "Fond Memories of Allen," pp. 146-147 (in) Morgan, Bill and Rosenthal, Bob (eds.). *Best Minds: A Tribute to Allen Ginsberg.* NY: Lospecchio Press, 1986.

Knight, Arthur and Kit (eds.). *Kerouac and the Beats: A Primary Sourcebook.* NY: Paragon House, 1988.

Knight, Brenda (ed.). *Women of the Beat Generation*. Berkeley: Conari Press, 1996.

Maher, Paul Jr. *Kerouac: The Definitive Biography*. Lanham: Taylor Trade Publishing, 2004.

Martelle, Scott. The Beat Goes On, pp. 4-13 (in) *Detroit News* (Feb. 19, 1989) Michigan Magazine section.

Miles, Barry. *Jack Kerouac: King of the Beats*. NY: Henry Holt, 1998.

Nicosia, Gerald. *Memory Babe: A Critical Biography*. NY: Grove Press, 1983.

Perrizo, Jim. "Frankie and Johnnie: A New York Memoir" (in) *Kerouac Connection*, no. 17 (Spring 1989).